CONNECTICUT OBSERVED:
Three Centuries of Visitors' Impressions
1676-1940

CONNECTICUT OBSERVED:

Three Centuries of Visitors' Impressions
1676-1940

Edited by Richard Buel, Jr.
and J. Bard McNulty

The Acorn Club
1899–1999

Thirty-fourth publication of
The Acorn Club
Designed by Teri Prestash, Red Barn Studios
Copyright © 1999 by The Acorn Club
ISBN 0-910721-09-2
Published by The Acorn Club
and the Connecticut Humanities Council
Library of Congress Catalog Card Number 99-72220

CONTENTS

COVER: VIEW OF NORWICH FROM THE WEST SIDE OF THE RIVER, BY FITZ HUGH LANE, LITHOGRAPH, 1849. THE CONNECTICUT HISTORICAL SOCIETY, HARTFORD.

"...wherever one has made up his mind to be buried, he would like to live in Norwich." (Page 127)

—*Samuel Adams Drake*

View of Norwich from the West Side of the River by FitzHugh Lane. Lithograph, 1849. (detail)

ACKNOWLEDGMENTS

The inspiration for this volume came from Christopher Bickford, late director of the Connecticut Historical Society. In the course of performing his curatorial duties, he became aware of an extensive travel literature in the Society's collections that spanned most of Connecticut's three-and-a-half-century history. Much of this literature was hidden away in obscure volumes long since forgotten by all but antiquarians. Bickford compiled a comprehensive bibliography, including material not in the possession of the Connecticut Historical Society, and brought it to the attention of the Acorn Club, of which he was then a member. The Club had been founded in 1899 to publish books of enduring value about Connecticut's history, and Bickford urged it to consider assembling an anthology of the best of the literature itemized in his bibliography.

The entire Club participated in a preliminary review of Bickford's bibliography, each member being instructed to choose the more interesting titles from those they were assigned. A committee consisting of J. Bard McNulty, Bruce Fraser and Bickford then assessed the significance of this winnowed sample. The committee was enthusiastic about the better exemplars of the genre. On the basis of its report, the Club committed itself to publishing a short anthology of Connecticut travel. Other Club members, including Richard Buel, Jr., Alice Delana, and Judith Schiff, joined the original committee members to select the final list of texts to be included. Still other club members, including Herbert Janick and Brian Rogers, helped draft individual introductions to each selection; the author of each introduction is identified by initials. Bard McNulty made arrangements for having the texts transcribed by Rachel Carlson, and assumed, with his wife, Marjorie, responsibility for the authenticity of the transcriptions. Brian Rogers and Oliver Jensen helped with proof reading, and William Robinson assisted with advice on the selection of illustrations. Illustrations were generously made available to the Club by the Connecticut Historical Society. Richard Buel made arrangements for design and printing. Ralph Elliot managed the legal side of the enterprise, advising on copyright and drafting an agreement with the volume's cosponsor, the Connecticut Humanities Council. Donald Engley contributed a brief history of the Acorn Club. Finally Richard Buel wrote introductions to each of the historical sections as well as the general introduction to the volume.

INTRODUCTION

The reports of visitors to Connecticut over the three-hundred-year span of this anthology provide cogent commentary on the history of the colony and the state. The personal quality of the observations reproduced here makes for lively reading. We see our state's past not abstractly but through the unmediated experience of others, which approaches as nearly as possible the way we would see it could we avail ourselves of a time machine. The selections cover the five major periods of the state's development: the colonial, the Revolutionary, the pre-Civil War, the post-Civil War, and the twentieth century. Four selections appear under each of these headings except the most recent one which is documented with only two selections. They are reproduced without any editorial intervention beyond the choice of passages that bear directly on Connecticut. Though most of the accounts in the anthology cannot be found in the average local library, obscure, hard-to-find texts appear alongside those by famous visitors like John Adams. Taken together they provide a brief, entertaining primer of Connecticut's history.

The accounts also comment on the distinctive character of Connecticut society. No author can record all that meets the eye. Inevitably some details and often whole fields of perception are screened out. If one writes from the vantage point of familiarity with one's subject, the temptation is to take many of its most salient features for granted. Since those are precisely the features which are the most relevant to defining the society's peculiar identity, this anthology contains only the impressions of non-residents.

All the authors included faced the task of giving tangible substance to what previously had been an abstract geographical designation. While none of the observations reprinted here approach the authority or breadth of Timothy Dwight's *Travel in New England and New York* (1810), what the non-Connecticut visitors lacked by way of comprehensive, systemic knowledge they more than made up for with the immediacy of their observations. In a sense the rightness or wrongness of their observations become less important than the freshness and vividness of their impressions.

The perceptions of the state by others has itself had a history. The earliest visitors tended to be critical of Connecticut's primitive rusticity, usually approaching it from other more developed regions, either at home or abroad. Many also reacted critically to its religious culture. Connecticut's blue laws regulating the way its inhabitants observed the sabbath drew particularly harsh criticism from those who were either not familiar with Puritan customs or who knew them all too well but nonetheless resented them. Finally, the Connecticut Yankee early on acquired the reputation for sharp economic practices.

With time the critical responses of visitors mellowed as enforcement of the laws regulating religious observances lapsed and a progressive society, itself the product of a dynamic economy, emerged during the nineteenth century. Later visitors customarily praised the beauty of the land and its natural resources. They also commented favorably on the state's growing towns, its distinctive institutions, particularly its churches and colleges, and the penchant of the industrious yankee for technological innovation. An increasing number of cultural luminaries possessed of both national and sometimes international reputations also received notice.

In the late nineteenth century, visitors came to see Connecticut as embodying a proper balance between industrial innovation and the preservation of a desired connection with the rural past. In other words, those aspects of the state's culture that initially attracted adverse commentary, especially its rustic quality, gradually became transformed into characteristics worthy of celebration. Increasingly, the visitors from this period presented the state as an ideal to which the rest of the nation and even

Europe should aspire. Only in the twentieth-century selections do the visitors' accounts begin to record the darker side of industrialism. In this way the anthology also records the degree to which the larger world beyond the state's borders was changing.

This volume is addressed to late twentieth-century readers. Each of the travel selections points to a way in which some aspect of the past survives in our present. But it also dramatizes the degree to which the past differs from the present. In that sense it puts the modern reader in a position analogous to that of past visitors. Just as they reacted to what was unfamiliar in Connecticut by recording it and in so doing defining themselves, so we respond to perceptions of the way in which the past differs from the present with heightened awareness of the present. In that sense the historian is like the traveler and the past is always about the present.

COLONIAL CONNECTICUT

During the colonial period most visitors to Connecticut who recorded their impressions of the colony in writing were of British descent and all were native English speakers. Though regional accents undoubtedly created problems in communicating, none of the authors of the following accounts experienced difficulty in understanding what was being said to them or in making themselves understood and none of them expected to experience such difficulty. All started from the common assumption that the most important thing binding the observer to the observed was what they shared in common.

The four accounts, however, are very different from each other. The differences are partially attributable to the varied purposes of the visitors. William Edmundson came to Connecticut accidentally, but interpreted the accident as a sign from God that he should bear witness to his Quakerism. Sarah Knight came to Connecticut on her way to New York. The alternative would have been a sea passage which, to judge from her fear of crossing streams, she meant to avoid at all costs. Alexander Hamilton, the Scottish physician, travelled through the colony to gratify his curiosity and recover his health. John Adams seemed to share the same motive as Hamilton, but he also used the occasion to take stock of the colony's resources and to introduce himself to some of its leaders.

The other reason why the accounts differ so radically relates to Connecticut's development between the mid-seventeenth century and the eve of the Revolution. Edmundson's observations at the end of King Philip's War portray a colony of isolated European settlements

surrounded by large expanses of threatening wilderness. Knight travelled through a denser environment of Europeans living along the coast
but had to accept primitive accommodations and amenities while in tran-
sit. By Hamilton's time the amenities for a traveller had caught up with
the increasing density of the population. Adams visited the state when
it was fully settled and had begun to export people to less developed
areas. He was drawn to Stafford by the reputation its springs were acquiring as a health resort. But the lack of stimulating company there
quickly led him to explore the older Connecticut River Valley towns
between Enfield and Middletown.

All the visitors responded to the deeply religious nature of the
colony's culture. Edmundson would not have bothered to bear the witness he did had he not believed the people of the colony shared his assumption that the Bible contained the explicit commands of God. Knight and
Hamilton had critical responses to the colony based in part on the religious orientation of Connecticut's people. For Knight this expressed itself
in the implicit judgment that the colony's culture was impoverished compared to what Boston and New York had to offer. Hamilton's response was
more explicit. He found the religious enthusiasms of the people distasteful
and complained when his travel plans were shaped by the colony's laws
about sabbath observance. Adams, who was native to the region though
not the colony, experienced no difficulty in accepting the religious
restrictions of the state as an expression of the New England way,
though he was interested in the more secular aspects of the society.

The era spanned by these accounts saw Connecticut develop at an
unprecedented rate. From tenuous settlements in the seventeenth century only marginally integrated in a larger market system, Connecticut
emerged in the eighteenth century as a significant player in a western
Atlantic economy centered on the West Indies. Despite the unsettling
effect of rapid growth, the colony also fabricated a corporate identity.
The following passages can be read as commentary on Connecticut's
evolution as the "Land of the Steady Habits."

৵৽ WILLIAM EDMUNDSON ৵৽

Wilfilliam Edmundson was born in the north of England in 1627.
Apprenticed a carpenter and joiner in York, he afterwards
served for a time in the Commonwealth Army during the English Civil
War. Eventually he was drawn to Quakerism, probably in response
to his military experiences. After meeting George Fox, he prosely-
tized actively for the Quakers, despite repeated persecutions, and in
1671 accompanied Fox on his journey to the West Indies and
North America. In August 1672 Edmundson was one of the three disciples of Fox who, after the departure of their leader from Rhode Island,
accepted Roger William's challenge to debate fourteen propositions
attacking the theological foundations of Quakerism. Afterwards
Edmundson returned to England, but came back to New England
in 1676 just as King Philip's War was coming to an end. Contracting
and recovering from an epidemic illness that beset the region in the
wake of the war, he embarked at Newport for New York. The journey proved a tempestuous one and his sloop was driven into New
London where Edmundson's attempt to hold a Quaker meeting was
obstructed by the authorities.

Setting out again for New York, the vessel lay pinned down by the
headwinds of an autumn storm for three days in an unidentified
Connecticut harbor. Edmundson construed the event as an unwelcome sign from God that he should proclaim the Quaker truth at Hartford.
The following passage recounts the way in which Edmundson came
to this conviction and his subsequent journey and witness. It high-
lights the religious uneasiness that accompanied King Philip's War
and suggests the fragility, at least at the level of popular belief, of
New England's Congregational orthodoxy.

R. B.

1676   Now whilst we were on board the sloop, came much upon me to go to New Hertford, a Chief Town in Connecticut Colony, which lay about Fifty Miles in the Country, through a great Wilderness, and very dangerous to travel, the Indians being in Arms, haunting those Parts, and killing many Christians: so it look'd frightful, that I, who was a Stranger in the Country, should undertake such a Journey in those perilous Times: but the service came close upon me, and I was under great Exercise of Mind about it, yet said nothing of it to any Man for some Days....

That Evening we weigh'd Anchor, and set sail, the Wind seemed something fair for us; but it still remain'd with me to go to New Hertford, yet it seemed hard to give up, to be expos'd to such Perils as seem'd to attend that Journey; but I kept it secret, thinking that the Lord might take it off me. We had sailed but about three Leagues when the Wind came strong ahead of us; that Night we had a Storm, and were glad to get a Harbour, where we lay some Days, the Wind blowing stiff against us. And the Hand of the Lord came heavy upon me, pressing me to go to New Hertford; so I gave up to the Will of God, whether to live or die. Then I told the Company, that I was the Cause, why they were so cross'd and detained in their Voyage. And I shew'd them, How the Lord had required me to go to New Hertford, and the Journey seeming perilous, I had delayed; but now must go, in Submission to the Will of God, whether I lived or died. The Owner of the Sloop wept, and the rest were amaz'd and tender.

Then James Fletcher would go with me: so we went on Shore, and bought each of us a Horse, and the next Morning took leave of our Sloop-Company; then went on our Journey without any Guide, except the Lord, and travel'd thro' a great Wilderness, which held us most of that Day's Journey. We travel'd hard, and by the Lord's gracious Assistance got that Night within four Miles of New-Hertford, where we lodg'd at an Ordinary, and the People were civil. I got up next Morning very early, it being the First Day of the Week, and went

Excerpted from William Edmundson, *A Quaker's Visit to Hartford in the Year 1676*, (ed. Frank D. Andrews), privately printed, Vineland, New Jersey, 1914 to Hertford on foot, leaving my Horse at the Ordinary, and desir'd James Fletcher to stay there, till he saw the Issue of my Service, for I expected at least a Prison at Hertford.

So getting there pretty soon in the Morning, the Town was about two Miles long; and I was moved to go to their Worship, I came to one great Meeting-House, but the Priest and People were not come to their Worship, it being early; and my Spirit was shut up from that Place. Then I was brought under great Exercise of Mind, fearing that the Lord was angry with me, and rejected my Service, for my Delay under this Exercise. I went on forward about Half a Mile, so came near to another great Meeting-House, and I found Openness in my Spirit to go thither, I was glad of the Lord's Countenance, tho' the People were not come yet to their Worship.

There was a brave River, where they built many Ships, about a Quarter of a Mile distant; thither I went, and sate down, until I saw People go to their Worship: when they were gather'd I went there, and stood in the Worship-House, near the Priest, until he had done his Service, then I spoke what the Lord gave me: They were moderate and quiet, and the Priest and the Magistrates went away, but many of the People staid, and I had good Service among them: when I had clear'd my Conscience we parted, and I went again towards the River-side. As I was going a Man call'd me to come to his House and dine with him: I stood a little and look'd at him, his Spirit seem'd to be deceitful, I ask'd him, If he would take Money for his Victuals? He said, No; then I told him, I would not eat with him. So I went to the Riverside again, and sate down, though I had not eaten any thing that Day.

After some time the Bells rung for their Afternoon Worship, and I was moved to go to the other Worship-House afore mention'd from which in the Morning my Spirit was shut up. So I went there, and the Priest and People were gather'd, having a Guard of Firelocks, for fear of the Indians coming upon them; whilst at their Worship I went in, and sounded an Alarm in the Dread of the Lord's Power, and they were startled, yet were kept down by the Lord's Power, in which I declared the way of Salvation unto them a pretty while; but after some time, by the Perswasions of the Priest, the Officers haled me out of the Worship-House, and hurt my Arm so that it bled; then they took me to the Guard of Firelocks upon a Hill.

And though it was a piercing cold Day, and I still Fasting, my Body also thin, by reason of the Sickness I had in Rhode-Island not long before, and other Exercises which I had travelled thro', yet the Lord's Power supported me, so that the Officer, who had me in Charge, first complained of the Sharpness of the Weather, and ask'd me How I could endure the Cold, for he was very cold? I told him, It was the Entertainment, that their great Professors of Religion in New-England afforded a Stranger, and yet profess'd the Scriptures to be their Rule, which commanded to entertain Strangers, and besides they had drawn my blood; So I shew'd him my Arm that was hurt; he seemed to be troubled, and excused their Magistrates. I told him, The Magistrates and Priests must answer for it to the Lord, for they were the cause of it: then he took me to an Inn, and presently the Room was fill'd with Professors: much Discourse we had, and the Lord strengthened me, and by his Spirit, brought many Scriptures to my Remembrance; so that Truth's Testimony was over them. As one Company went away another came.

When they were foil'd, a Preacher amongst the Baptists took up the Argument against Truth, charging Friends with holding a great Error, [which was] That every Man had a Measure of the Spirit of Christ; and would know, If I held the same error? I told him, That was no Error, for the Scriptures witnessed to it plentifully. He said, He denied, that the World had received a measure of the Spirit, but Believers had received it. I told him that the Apostle said, A manifestation of the Spirit was given to every one to profit withal. He said, That was meant to every one of the believers. I told him, Christ had enlightened every one that came into the World, with the Light of his Spirit:

He said, That was every one of the Believers that came into the World: and as I brought him Scriptures, he still applied them to the Believers, saying, There was the Ground of our Error, in applying that to every Man which properly belonged to Believers. Then the Lord by his good Spirit brought to my Mind the Promise of our Saviour, [which he told his Disciples of his going away] That he would send the Comforter, the Spirit of Truth, that should convince the World of Sin, and should guide his Disciples into all Truth: Thus the same Spirit of Truth, that leads Believers into all Truth, convinces the World of Sin. So thou must grant, that all have received it, or else shew from the Scriptures a Select Number of Believers; and besides them a World of Believers that hath the Spirit, also another World of Unbelievers, that hath no Measure of the Spirit to convince them of Sin.

Here the Lord's Testimony came over him, so that he was stop'd, and many sober Professors, who staid to see the End, acquiesc'd therewith, and said, indeed, Mr. Rogers, the Man is in the right, for you must find a Select Number of Believers, besides a World that hath a Measure of the Spirit, that convinces them of Sin, and a World that hath not the Spirit, so not convinc'd of Sin: this you must do, or grant the Argument. He was silent, and the People generally satisfied in that matter, their Understandings being open'd; so they took their leave of me very lovingly, it being late in the Night.

When they were gone, I desired the Woman of the House to boil me a little Milk, for that Day I had not eaten. The Baptist Rogers (aforesaid) lodg'd there that Night, but liv'd Fifty Miles off, and was Pastor to those Seven-Day-Sabbath People, that I had been with above a Week before near New London. The People of this House where we lodged being Presbyterians, I call'd the Baptist from them into another room: he told me where he liv'd, and what People he was Pastor to. I told him, I was with his Hearers, and they were loving and tender. He also acquainted me, he was summon'd to Hertford, to appear before the Assembly that then sate, who had taken away his Wife from him, whom he had married some Years ago, before he was of the Perswasion that he now was of. And since he became a Baptist, her Father, being an Elder of the Presbyterians, was set violently against him, and endeavoured to divorce his Daughter from him, [though he had two Children by her] for some ill Fact he had committed before he was her Husband, and whilst he was one of their Church; whereof, under Sorrow and Trouble of Mind, he had acquainted her, and she had divulged the same to her Father; for which, he said, they had taken away his Wife. I ask'd, How he could join with them in opposing me; and at such a time when I was but One, being a stranger, and they Abundant in Opposition? Also, Whether it was not unmanly to do so? But it being late, I desir'd some further Discourse with him in the Morning, which he assented to; but although I was up before the Sun rose, he had gone away before.

I sent to the Officer, that had the Charge of me the Day before, to know, if he had any further to do with me, who said, I might go when and where I pleas'd. So I paid the people for my Nights Lodging, and being clear of the Service there, I went towards the Place where I left James Fletcher and our Horses; in the mean time James Fletcher came another way to look for me: thus we miss'd of one another. When he came to Hertford, he heard by several where I was gone, and so came back, and told me, That I had set all the Town a Talking of Religion.

ᏋᏊ SARA KEMBLE KNIGHT ᎧᏋᏊ

S arah Kemble Knight was born in 1666, the daughter of a Boston merchant, Thomas Kemble and Elizabeth Trerice. She married an older man who was a sea captain and who was absent from their home for most of their marriage. Sarah quickly got used to acting for herself and, after her father's death in 1689, became the head of the household.

She ran a boarding school and taught herself to be proficient both as a scrivener and in settling estates at law. The journal, from which the passage below is extracted, recounts an overland journey to New Haven and New York that she undertook in October 1704 to settle the affairs of a recently deceased cousin.

When women traveled in this era, they usually did so in the company of men who were their kin. Though Knight was on her own, she had no intention of being an exception to that rule, and she carefully procured a male escort at every stage of her journey. The physical environment through which Knight moved failed to claim much of her attention. October 5-7 old style should have corresponded to the height of the autumn foliage, but she took no notice of it. Instead, she regards nature as creating a series of unwelcome obstacles to be surmounted. At no point does she express real pleasure in the prospect presented to her.

Knight was much more sensitive to her human environment. Most of her journal describes her traveling companions and the people she encountered along the way and reports, often in quaint dialogue, what was said to her as well as her response to it. The passage below picks up as Knight enters Stonington from Rhode Island.

R. B.

1704 I ridd on very slowly thro' Stoningtown, where the rode was very stony and uneven. I asked the fellow, as we went, divers questions of the place and way, &c. I being arrived at my country Saxtons, at Stonington, was very well accommodated both as to victuals and Lodging, the only Good of both I had found since my setting out. Here I heard there was an old man and his Daughter to come that way, bound to N. London; and being now destitute of a Guide, gladly waited for them, being in so good a harbour, and accordingly...

Excerpted from *The Journal of Madam Knight*, (ed. George Parker Winship), Boston, Small, Maynard, & Company, 1920.

Thirsday, Octobrye 5th,

…about 3 in the afternoon, I set forward with neighbor Polly and Jemima, a Girl about 18 Years old, who hee said he had been to fetch out of the Narragansetts, and said they had Rode thirty miles that day, on a sory lean Jade, wth only a Bagg under her for a pillion, which the poor Girl often complain'd was very uneasy.

Wee made Good speed along, wch made poor Jemima make many a sow'r face, the mare being a very hard trotter; and after many a hearty and bitter Oh, she at length Low'd out: Lawful Heart father! this bare mare hurts mee Dingeely, I'me direfull sore I vow; with many words to that purpose: poor Child sais Gaffer-she us't to serve your mother so. I don't care how mother us't to do, quoth Jemima, in a passionate tone. At which the old man Laught, and kik't his Jade o' the side, which made her Jolt ten times harder.

About seven that Evening, we come to New London Ferry: here, by reason of a very high wind, we mett with great difficulty in getting over. —the Boat tos't exceedingly, and our Horses capper'd at a very surprizing Rate, and set us all in a fright; especially poor Jemima, who desired her father to say so jack to the Jade, to make her stand. But the careless parent, taking no notice of her repeated desires, She Rored out in a Passionate manner: Pray suth father, Are you deaf? Say so Jack to the Jade, I tell you. The Dutiful Parent obey's; saying so Jack, so Jack, as gravely as if hee'd bin to saying Catechise after Young Miss, who with her fright look't of all coullors in ye Rain Bow.

Being safely arrived at the house of Mrs. Prentices in N. London, I treated neighbour Polly and daughter for their divirting company, and bid them farewell; and between nine and ten at night waited on the Revd Mr. Gurdon Saltonstall, minister of the town, who kindly Invited me to Stay that night at his house, where I was very handsomely and plentifully treated and Lodg'd; and made good the Great Character I had before heard concerning him: viz. That hee was the most affable, courteous, Genero's and best of men.

Friday, Octor 6th.

I got up very early, in Order to hire somebody to go with mee to New Haven, being in Great parplexity at the thoughts of proceeding alone; which my most hospitable entertainer observing, himselfe went, and soon return'd wth a young Gentleman of the town, who he could confide in to Go with mee; and about eight this morning, wth Mr. Joshua Wheeler my new Guide, takeing leave of this worthy Gentleman, Wee advanced on towards Seabrook. The Rodes all along this way are very bad, Incumbred wth Rocks and mountainos passages, wch were very disagreeable to my tired carcass; but we went on with a moderate pace wch made ye Journy more pleasent. But after about eight miles Rideing, in going over a Bridge under wch the River Run very swift, my hors stumbled, and very narrowly 'scaped falling over into the watcr; wch extreemly frightened mee. But through God's Goodness I met with no harm, and mounting agen, in about half a miles Rideing, come to an ordinary, were well entertained by a woman of about seventy and vantage, but of as Sound Intellectuals as one of seventeen. Shee entertain'd Mr. Wheeler wth some passages of a Wedding awhile ago at a place hard by, the Brides-Groom being about her Age or something above, Saying his Children was dreadfully against their fathers marrying, wch she condemned them extreemly for.

From hence wee went pretty briskly forward, and arriv'd at Saybrook ferry about two of the Clock afternoon; and crossing it, wee call'd at an Inn to Bait, (foreseeing we should not have such another Opportunity till we come to Killingsworth.) Landlady come in, with her hair about her ears, and hands at full pay scratching. Shee told us shee had some mutton wch shee would broil, wch I was glad to hear; But I supose forgot to wash her scratches; in a little time shee brot it in; but it being pickled, and my Guide said it smelt strong of head sause, we left it, and pd sixpence a piece for our Dinners, wch was only smell.

So wee putt forward with all speed, and about seven at night come to Killingsworth, and were tollerably well with Travillers fare, and Lodgd there that night.

Saturday, Oct. 7th,

we sett out early in the Morning, and being something unacquainted wth the way, having ask't it of some wee mett, they told us wee must Ride a mile or two and turne down a Lane on the Right hand; and by their Direction wee Rode on but not Yet comeing to ye turning, we mett a Young fellow and ask't him how farr it was to the Lane which turn'd down towards Guilford. Hee said wee must Ride a little further, and turn down by the Corner of uncle Sams Lott. My Guide vented his Spleen at the Lubber; and we soon after came into the Rhode, and keeping still on, without any thing further Remarkabell, about two a clock afternoon we arrived at New Haven, where I was received with all Posible Respects and civility. Here I discharged Mr. Wheeler with a reward to his satisfaction, and took some time to rest after so long and toilsome a Journey; and Inform'd myselfe of the manners and customs of the place, and at the same time employed myselfe in the afair I went there upon.

They are Govern'd by the same Laws as wee in Boston, (or little differing,) thr' out this whole Colony of Connecticot, And much the same way of Church Government, and many of them good, Sociable people, and I hope Religious too: but a little too much Independence in their principalls, and, as I have been told, were formerly in their Zeal very Riggid in their Administrations towards such as their Lawes made Offenders, even to a harmless Kiss or Innocent merriment among Young people. Whipping being a frequent and counted an easy Punishment, about wch as other Crimes, the Judges were absolute in their Sentances.

...on training dayes The Youth divert themselves by Shooting at the Target, as they call it, (but it very much resembles a pillory,) where hee that hitts neerest the white has some yards of Red Ribbon presented him wch being tied to his hattband, the two ends streeming down his back, he is Led away in Triumph, wth great applause, as the winners of the Olympiack Games. They generally marry very young:

the males oftener as I am told under twentie than above; they generally make public weddings, and have a way something singular (as they say) in some of them, viz. Just before Joyning hands the Bridegroom quitts the place, who is soon followed by the Bridesmen, and as it were, dragg'd back to duty—being the reverse to ye former practice among us, to steal ms Pride.

There are great plenty of Oysters all along by the sea side, as farr as I Rode in the Collony, and those very good. And they Generally lived very well and comfortably in their famelies. But too Indulgent (especially ye farmers) to their slaves: sufering too great familiarity from them, permitting ym to sit at Table and eat with them, (as they say to save time,).... They told me that there was a farmer lived nere the Town where I lodgd who had some difference wth his slave, concerning something the master had promised him and did not punctualy perform; wch caused some hard words between them; But at length they put the matter to Arbitration and Bound themselves to stand to the award of such as they named—wch done, the Arbitrators Having heard the Allegations of both parties, Order the master to pay 40s to black face, and acknowledge his fault. And so the matter ended: the poor master very honestly standing to the award.

There are every where in the Towns as I passed, a Number of Indians the Natives of the Country, and are the most salvage of all the salvages of that kind that I had ever Seen: little or no care taken (as I heard upon enquiry) to make them otherwise. They have in some places Landes of their owne, and Govern'd by Law's of their own making;—they marry many wives and at pleasure put them away, and on the least dislike or fickle humour, on either side, saying *stand away* to one another is a sufficient Divorce. And indeed those uncomely *Stand aways* are too much in Vougue among the English in this (Indulgent Colony) as their Records plentifully prove, and that on very trivial matters, of which some have been told me, but are not proper to be Related by a Female pen, tho some of that foolish sex have had too large a share in the story.

If the natives committ any crime on their own precincts among them-selves, ye English takes no Cognezens of. But if on the English ground, they are punishable by our Laws. They mourn for their Dead by blacking their faces, and cutting their hair, after an Awkerd and fright-full manner; But can't bear You should mention the names of their dead Relations to them: they trade most for Rum, for wch theyd hazzard their very lives; and the English fit them Generally as well, by seasoning it plentifully with water.

They give the title of merchant to every trader; who Rate their Goods according to the time and specie they pay in: *viz.* Pay, mony, Pay as mony, and trusting. *Pay* is Grain, Pork, Beef, &c. at the prices sett by the General Court that Year; *mony* is pieces of Eight, Ryalls, or Boston or Bay shillings (as they call them,) or Good hard money, as sometimes silver coin is termed by them; also Wampon, vizt. Indian beads wch serves for change. *Pay as mony* is provisions, as aforesd one Third cheaper then as the Assembly or the Genel Court sets it; and *Trust* as they and the mercht agree for time.

Now, when the buyer comes to ask for a comodity, sometimes before the merchant answers that he has it, he sais, is *Your pay redy?* Perhaps the Chap Reply's Yes: what do You pay in? say's the merchant. The buyer having answered, then the price is set; as suppose he wants a sixpenny knife, in pay it is 12d—in pay as money eight pence, and hard money its own price, *viz.* 6d. It seems a very Intricate way of trade and what *Lex Mercatoria* had not thought of.

Being at a merchants house, in comes a tall country fellow, wth his alfogeos full of Tobacco; for they seldom Loose their Cudd, but keep Chewing and Spitting as long as they'r eyes are open,—he advanc't to the middle of the Room, makes an Awkward Nodd, and spitting a Large deal of Aromatick Tincture, he gave a scrape with his shovel like shoo, leaving a small shovel full of dirt on the floor, made a full stop, Hugging his own pretty Body with his hands under his arms, Stood staring rown'd him, like a Catt let out of a Baskett. At last, like the creature Balaam Rode on, he opened his mouth and said: have You any Ribinen for Hatbands to sell I pray? The Questions and Answers about the pay being past, the Ribin is bro't and opened. Bumpkin Simpers, cryes its confounded Gay I vow; and beckning to the door, in comes Jone Tawdry, dropping about 50 curtsees, and stands by him: hee shows her the Ribin. *Law You*, sais shee, *its right Gent*, do You, take it, *tis dreadfull pretty.* Then she enquires, *have You any hood silk I pray?* Wch being brought and bought, Have You any *thred silk to sew it wth* says shee, wch being accomodated wth they Departed. They Generaly stand after they come in a great while speachless, and sometimes dont say a word till they are askt what they want, which I Impute to the Awe they stand in of the merchants, who they are constantly almost Indebted to; and must take what they bring without Liberty to choose for themselves; but they serve them as well, making the merchants stay long enough for their pay.

We may Observe here the great necessity and bennifitt both of Education and Conversation; for these people have as Large a portion of mother witt, and sometimes a Larger, than those who have bin brought up in Citties; But for want of emprovements, Render themselves almost Ridiculos, as above. I should be glad if they would leave such follies, and am sure all that Love Clean Houses (at least) would be glad on't too.

They are generaly very plain in their dress, throuout all ye Colony, as I saw, and follow one another in their modes; that You may know where they belong, especially the women, meet them where you will.

Their chief Red Letter day is St. Election, wch is annualy Observed according to Charter, to choose their Govenr: a blessing they can never be thankfull enough for, as they will find, if ever it be their hard fortune to loose it. The present Govenor in Conecticott is the Honble John Winthrop Esq. A Gentlemen of an Ancient and Honourable Family, whose Father was Govenor here sometimes before, and his Grand

father had bin Govr of the Massachusetts. This gentlemen is a very cur-
teous and afable person, much Given to Hospitality, and has by his Good
services Gain'd the affection of the people as much as any who had bin
before him in that post.

Decr 6th.

Being by this time well Recruited and rested after my Journy, my business lying unfinished by some concerns at New York depending there-
upon, my Kinsman, Mr. Thomas Trowbridge of New Haven, must
needs take a Journy there before it could be accomplished, I resolved
to go there in company wth him, and a man of the town wch I engaged
to wait on me there. Accordingly, Dec. 6th we set out from New Haven,
and about 11 same morning came to Stratford ferry; wch crossing, about
two miles on the other side Baited our horses and would have eat a
morsell ourselves, But the Pumpkin and Indian mixt Bred had such
an Aspect, and the Bare-legg'd Punch so awkerd or rather Awfull a
sound, that we left both, and proceeded forward, and about seven
at night come to Fairfield, where we met with good entertainment
and Lodg'd; and early next morning set forward to Norowalk, from
its halfe Indian name *North-walk*, when about 12 at noon we arrived,
and Had a Dinner of Fryed Venison, very savoury. Landlady wanting some pepper in the seasoning, bid the Girl hand her the spice
in the little *Gay* cupp on ye shelfe. From hence we Hasted towards
Rye, walking and Leading our Horses neer a mile together, up a prodi-
gios high Hill; and so Riding till about nine at night, and there arrived
and took up our Lodgings at an ordinary, wch a French family kept.
Here being very hungry, I desired a fricasee, wch the Frenchman under-
takeing, mannaged so contrary to my notion of Cookery, that I hastened to Bed superless.

❧ ALEXANDER HAMILTON ☙

*A*lexander Hamilton was born near Edinburgh in 1712, the younger son of Dr. William Hamilton, a professor of Divinity and Principal of the University there. After taking a degree in medicine at Edinburgh in 1737, he emigrated to Annapolis, Maryland in 1739, and set up as a doctor. Four years later, in the spring of 1743, he contracted a pulmonary disease, probably tuberculosis. This led him seriously to consider returning to his native Scotland. He had recovered sufficiently by the following autumn, however, to postpone his return indefinitely. He decided to spare himself the heat of the next Chesapeake summer by touring the colonies to the northward.

On May 30, 1744 he and his servant, Dromo, set off for Philadelphia, New York, and New England. In addition to a side trip to Albany and its environs, his travels took him to faraway York, Maine. His initial introduction to New England was by boat from eastern Long Island to New London in mid-July, covered in the first brief passage. From there he made his way by Stonington to Rhode Island and Boston. He did not return to Connecticut until the end of August, retracing his route from Stonington to New London and then proceeding down the coast to New York, as described in the second passage.

Hamilton passed through Connecticut at the beginning of King George's War against the French and, more significantly, shortly after the high point of religious enthusiasm engendered by the Great Awakening. He had little sympathy for what he regarded as Puritan bigotry and, though a sociable man by inclination, found few congenial spirits in the colony to converse with. Consequently, his account is richer in physical than human detail. Nonetheless, taken in conjunction with Sarah Kemble Knight's journal of her travels, it provides an interesting measure of the degree to which the colony had developed in the intervening forty years.

R. B.

1744

[First visit arriving from eastern Long Island on the evening of July 13, 1744] We arrived in the harbour att New London att half an hour after 6 and put up att Duchand's the Sign of the Anchor. The town of New London is irregularly built along the water side, in length about a mile. There is in it one Presbyterian meeting and one church. 'Tis just such another desolate expensive town as Annapolis in Maryland, the houses being mostly wood. The inhabitants were allarmed this night att a sloop that appeared to be rowing up into the harbour, they having heard a little before a firing of guns out in the Sound and seen one vessell, as they thought, give chase to another. There was a strange clamour and crowd in the street, chiefly of women. The country station sloop lay in the harbour, who, when she was within shot, sent a salute, first one gun, sharp shot, but the advancing sloop did not strike; then she bestowed upon her another, resolving next to proceed to a volley; but att the second shot, which whistled thro' her rigging, she struck and made answer that it was one Captain Trueman from Antegua. Then the people's fears were over, for they imagined it was old Morpang, the French rover, who in former times used to plunder these parts when he wanted provision.

Stonington

Saturday, July 14th. We departed New London att seven a'clock in the morning, crossing the ferry, and rid eight miles thro a very stonny rough road where the stones upon each hand of us seemed as large as houses, and the way it self a mere rock. This is properly enough called Stonnington. We breakfasted att one Major William's and proceeded 10 miles farther to Thomson's where we baited our horses. Here we met one Captain Noise, a dealer in cattle, whose name and character seemed pritty well to agree, for he talked very loud, joaked and laughed heartily att nothing. The landlady here was a queer old woman, an enormous heap of fat. She had some daughters and maids

Excerpted from *Gentleman's Progress; The Itenerarium of Dr. Alexander Hamilton*, 1744 , edited by Carl Bridenbaugh. Published for the Institute of Early American History and Culture. Copyright © 1948 by The University of North Carolina Press. Used by permission of the publisher.

whom she called by comical names. There was Thankfull, Charity, Patience, Comfort, Hope, etc.

[Returning from the east, August 25, 1744] In ... Rhode Island and Providence you may travell without molestation upon Sunday, which you cannot do in Connecticut or the Massachusets province without a pass, because here they are not agreed what day of the week the sabbath is to be kept, some observing it upon Saturday and others upon Sunday.

I dined att Williams's att Stonington with a Boston merchant named Gardiner and one Boyd, a Scotch Irish

pedlar. The pedlar seemed to understand his business to a hair. He sold some dear bargains to Mrs. Williams, and while he smoothed her up with palaber, the Bostoner amused her with religious cant ... Our conversation att dinner was a medley; Gardiner affected much learning and pedlar talked of trade.

I left Williams's about half an hour after 3, and crossing the ferry a little after 5 o'clock, I arrived att New London and put up att Duchand's att the Sign of the Anchor. I did not know till now that I had any relations in this town; a parcell of children, as I rid up the lane, saluted me with "How d'ye, unkle? Welcome to town, uncle."

Sunday, August 26. I stayed att home most of the forenoon and was invited to dine with Collector Lechmere, son to the surveyor att Boston. There was att table there one Dr. Goddard and an old maid whom they called Miss Katy, being a great fat woman with a red face, as much like an old maid as a frying pan. There sat by her a young modest looking lady dressed in black whom Mr. Lechmere called Miss Nansy, and next to her, a walnut coloured, thin woman, sluttishly dressed and very hard favoured. These ladys went to meeting after dinner, and we three sat drinking of punch and telling of droll storys.

I went home att 6 o'clock, and Deacon Green's son came to see me. He entertained me with the history of the behaviour of one Davenport, a fanatick preacher there who told his flock in one of his enthusiastic rhapsodies that in order to be saved they ought to burn all their idols.

They began this conflagration with a pile of books in the public street, among which were Tillotson's Sermons, Beveridge's Thoughts, Drillincourt on Death, Sherlock and many other excellent authors, and sung psalms and hymns over the pile while it was a burning. They did not stop here, but the women made up a lofty pile of hoop petticoats, silk gowns, short cloaks, cambrick caps, redheeld shoes, fans, necklaces, gloves, and other such aparrell, and what was merry enough, Davenport's own idol with which he topped the pile, was a pair of old, wore out, plush breaches. But this bone fire was happily prevented by one more moderate than the rest, who found means to perswade them that making such a sacrifice was not necessary for their salvation, and so every one carried of[f] their idols again, which was lucky for Davenport who, had fire been put to the pile, would have been obliged to strutt about bare-arsed, for the devil another pair of breeches had he but these same old plush ones which were going to be offered up as an expiatory sacrifise. Mr. Green took his leave of me att 10 o'clock, and I went to bed.

Monday, August 27. After visiting Deacon Green this morning and drinking tea with him and his wife, he gave me a paquet for his son Jonas att Annapolis. The old man was very inquisitive about the state of religion with us, what kind of ministers we had, and if the people were much addicted to godliness. I told him that the ministers minded hogsheads of tobacco more than points of doctrine, either orthodox or hetrodox, and that the people were very prone to a certain religion called *self interest.*

I left New London betwixt eight and 9 o'clock in the morning and crossed Hantick [Niantic] Ferry, or the Gutt, a little before ten. This is an odd kind of a ferry, the passage across it not being above 50 paces wide, and yet the inlett of water here from the Sound is near three quarters of a mile broad. This is occasioned by a long narrow point or promontory of hard sand and rock, att its broadest part not above 12 paces over, which runs out from the western towards the eastern shore of this inlett and is above half a mile long, so leaves but a small gutt where the tide runs very rapid and fierce. The skeow that crosses here goes by a rope which is fixed to a stake att each side of the Gutt, and this skeow is fastened to the main rope by an iron ring which slides upon it, else the rapidity of the tide would carry skeow and passengers and all away.

A little after I passed this ferry I rid close by an Indian town upon the left hand situated upon the brow of the hill. This town is called Nantique and consists of 13 or 14 hutts or wig-wams made of bark.

I passed over a bridge in vary bad repair for which I payed eight pence toll, which here is something more than a penny farthing sterling, and coming down to Seabrook Ferry upon Connecticut River, I waited there 3 or 4 hours att the house of one Mather before I could get passage. The wind blew so hard att north-west with an ebb tide which, the ferrymen told me, would have carried us out into the Sound had we attempted to pass.

Mather and I had some talk about the opinions lately broached here in religion. He seemed a man of some solidity and sense and condemned Whitefield's conduct in these parts very much. After dinner there came in a rabble of clowns who fell to disputing upon points of divinity as learnedly as if they had been professed theologues. 'Tis strange to see how this humour prevails, even among the lower class of the people here. They will talk so pointedly about justification, sanctification, adoption, regeneration, repentance, free grace, reprobation, original sin, and a thousand other such pritty, chimerical knick knacks as if they had done nothing but studied divinity all their life time and perused all the lumber of the scholastic divines, and yet the fellows look as much, or rather more, like clowns than the very riff-raff of our Maryland planters. To talk in this dialect in our parts would be like Greek, Hebrew, or Arabick.

I met with an old paralytic man in this house named Henderson who let me know that he had travelled the world in his youthfull days and had been in Scotland and lived some years in Edinburgh. He condemned much the conduct of the late enthusiasts here, by which he put some of our clowns in company in a frett, but the old man regarded them not, going on with his discourse, smoking his pipe, and shaking his grey locks. I was very much taken with his conversation, and he, seemingly, with mine, for he gave me many a hearty shake by the hand att parting and wished me much prosperity, health, and a safe return home.

I crossed the ferry att 5 o'clock. This river of Connecticut is navigable for 50 miles up the country. Upon it are a good many large trading towns, but the branches of the river run up above 200 miles. We could see the town of Seabrook [Saybrook] below us on the western side of the river. I lodged this night att one Mrs. Lay's a widow woman, who keeps a good house upon the road about 6 miles from Seabrook. I had much difficulty to find the roads upon this side Connecticut River. They wind and turn so much and are divided into such a number of small paths.

I find they are not quite so scrupulous about bestowing titles here as in Maryland. My landlady goes here by the name of Madam Lay. I cannot tell for what, for she is the homliest piece both as to mein, make, and dress that ever I saw, being a little round shouldered woman, pale faced and wrinkly, clothed in the coarsest home spun cloth; but it is needless to dispute her right to the title since we know many upon whom it is bestowed who have as little right as she.

Tuesday, August 28. I departed Lay's att seven in the morning and rid some miles thro' a rockey high land, the wind blowing pritty sharp and cool att northwest.

A little after eight o'clock I passed thro' Killingsworth, a small town pleasantly situated. I breakfasted att one Scran's about half way betwixt Killingsworth and Gilfoord. This is a jolly old man, very fat and pursy, and very talkative and full of history. He had been an American soldier in Q. Anne's War and had travelled thro' most of the continent of North America....

Going from this house I passed thro' Gilfoord att eleven o'clock in company of an old man whom I overtook upon the road. He showed me a curious stone bridge within a quarter of a mile of this town. It lay over a small brook and was one intire stone about 10 foot long, six broad, and 8 or 10 inches thick, being naturally bent in the form of an arch without the help of a chisell to cut it into that shape. "Observe here, sir," says the old man, "you may ride 1000 miles and not meet with such a stone." Gilford is a pritty town built upon a pleasant plain. In it there is a meeting, upon the steeple of which is a publick clock.

I came to Branfoord, another scattered town built upon high rocky ground, a little after one o'clock, where I dined att the house of one Frazer. Going from thence I passed thro' a pleasant, delightfull part of the country, being a medley of fine green plains, and little rockey and woody hills, caped over, as it were, with bushes.

I crossed Newhaven Ferry betwixt 4 and 5 o'clock in the afternoon. This is a pleasant navigable river that runs thro a spacious green plain into the Sound. I arrived in Newhaven att 5 o'clock, where I put up att one Monson's att the Sign of the Half Moon. There is but little good liquor to be had in the publick houses upon this road. A man's horses are better provided for than himself, but he pays dear for it. The publick house keepers seem to be somewhat wild and shy when a stranger calls. It is with difficulty you can get them to speak to you, show you a room, or ask you what you would have, but they will gape and stare when you speak as if they were quite astonished.

Newhaven is a pritty large, scattered town laid out in squares, much in the same manner as Philadelphia, but the houses are sparse and thin sowed. It stands on a large plain, and upon all sides (excepting the south which faces the Sound) it is inclosed with ranges of little hills as old Jerusalem was according to the topographicall descriptions of that city. The burying place is in the center of the town just faceing the college [Yale], which is a wooden building about 200 foot long and three stories high, in the middle front of which is a little cupula with a clock upon it. It is not so good a building as that att Cambridge, nor are there such a number of students. It was the gift of a private gentleman to this place.

Wednesday, August 29th. I set out from Monson's a little after 7 o'clock and rid a tollerable good road to Millford. Before I came there I was overtaken by a young man who asked me severall questions according to country custom, such as where I was going and whence I came, and the like, to all which I gave answers just as impertinent as the questions were themselves. I breakfasted in Millford att one Gibb's, and while I was there the post arrived so that there came great crowds of the politicians of the town to read the news, and we had plenty of orthographicall blunders. We heard of some prizes taken by the Philadelphia privateers. Millford is a large scattered town situated upon a large pleasant plain.

I went from here in company of a young man and crossed Stratford Ferry att eleven o'clock and was obliged to call att Stratfoord, my grey horse having lost a shoe. I stayed there sometime att one Benjamin's who keeps a tavern in the town. There I met a deal of company and had many questions asked me. Stratfoord is a pleasant little town prittily situated upon a rising ground within half a mile of a navigable river that runs into the Sound. In this town is one Presbyterian meeting and one church, both new buildings. The church is built with some taste and elegance, having large arched sash windows and a handsom spire or steeple att the west end of it.

My young man rid with me till I came within 5 miles of Fairfield, which is another town in which is an octogonall church or meeting built of wood like that of Jamaica upon Long Island, upon the cupolo of which is a publick clock. The roads between this town and Norwalk are exceeding rough and stonny, and the stones are very full of a glittering isinglass. There is a river on the west side of this town which runs into the Sound. I forded it att high water when pritty deep.

Within three miles and a half of Norwalk is another river called by the Indian name of Sagatick. This I forded att low tide. I dined att one Taylor's here. My landlord was an old man of 70. He understanding from my boy that I was a doctor from Maryland and having heard that some of the doctors there were wonder workers in practice, he asked my advice about a cancer which he had in his lip. I told him there was one Bouchelle in Maryland who pretended to cure every disease by the help of a certain water which he made, but as for my part, I knew of no way of curing a cancer but by extirpation or cutting it out.

I arrived att Norwalk att seven o'clock att night. This town is situated in a bottom midst a grove of trees. You see the steeple shoot up among the trees about half a mile before you enter the town and before you can see any of the houses. While I was att Taylor's the children were frightened att my negroe, for here negroe slaves are not so much in use as with us, their servants being chiefly bound or indentured Indians. The child asked if that negroe was a coming to eat them up. Dromo indeed wore a voracious phiz, for having rid 20 miles without eating, he grinned like a crocodile and showed his teeth most hideously.

Betwixt Taylor's and Norwalk I met a caravan of 18 or 20 Indians. I put up att Norwalk att one Beelding's, and as my boy was taking off the saddles, I could see one half of the town standing about him making enquiry about his master.

I was disturbed this night by a parcell of roaring fellows that came rumbling up stairs to go to bed in the next room. They beat the walls with their elbows as if they had had a mind to batter down the house, being inspired, I suppose by the great god Bacchus. A certain horse jockey in the company had a voice as strong as a trumpet, and Stentor like, he made the house ring. "Damme," says he, "if you or any man shall have the jade for 100 pounds. The jade is as good a jade as ever wore curb." (It is customary here to call both horses and mares by the name of jades.) I wished he and his jade both once and again at the devil for disturbing my rest, for just as I was a dropping asleep again he uttered some impertinence with his Stentorian voice which made me start and waked me. My rest was broken all that night, and waking suddenly from a confused dream about my horse dropping dead under me in the road, I imagined I heard somebody breath very high in the bed by me. I thought perhaps that my friend Stentor had thought fit to come there and felt about with my arms but could discover nothing but the bed cloths tho the sound continued very distinct in my ears for about a minute after I was broad awake, and then it dyed away by degrees. This, with some people, would have procured the house a bad name of its being haunted with spirits.

Thursday, August 30. I left Norwalk att 7 in the morning and rid 10 miles of stonny road, crossing severall brooks and rivulets that run into the Sound, till I came to Stanford. A little before I reached this town, from the top of a stonny hill, I had a large open view or prospect of the country westward. The greatest part of it seemed as it were covered with a white crust of stone. For the country here is exceeding rockey, and the roads very rough, rather worse than Stonnington. I breakfasted att Stanford att one Ebenezar Weak's. In this town I saw a new church, which is now abuilding, the steeple of which was no sooner finished than it was all tore to pieces by lightning in a terrible thunder storm that happened here upon the first day of August in the afternoon. I observed the rafters of the steeple split from top to bottom, and the wooden pins or trunells that fastened the joints half drawn out.

While I was att breakfast att Weak's, there came in a crazy old man who complained much of the hardness of the times and of pains in his back and belly. "Lack a day for poor old Joseph!" said the landlady. A little after him came in one Captain Lyon, living att Rye Bridge. He wore an affected air of wisdom in his phiz and pretended to be a very knowing man in the affairs of the world. ... Most of his knowledge was pedantry, being made up of common place sentences and trite proverbs. I asked him if I should have his company down the road. He replied that he would be glad to wait on me, but had an appointment to eat some roast pigg with a neighbour of his which would detain him till the afternoon. So I departed the town without him.

I rode a stonny and hilly road to Horseneck and overtook an old man who rid a sorrell mare with a colt following her. He told me he was obliged to ride slow for fear of losing the colt, for sometimes the creature strayed behind, meeting with jades upon the way. He said he had been traveling the country for 3 weeks visiting his children and grandchildren who were settled for 50 miles round him. He told me he had had 21 sons and daughters of which 19 were now alive, and 15 of them married and had children; and yet he did not marry himself till 27 years of age and was now only 72 years old. This old man called in att a house about 2 miles from Horseneck where he said there lived a friend of his. An old fellow with a mealy hat came to the door and received him with a "How d'ye, old friend Jervis?" So I parted with my company.

I passed thro Horseneck, a scattered town, att half an hour after eleven a clock and passed over Rye Bridge att 12, the boundary of Connecticut and York government, after having rid 155 miles in Connecticut government.

"Farewell, Connecticut," said I, as I passed along the bridge. "I have had a surfeit of your ragged money, rough roads, and enthusiastick people."

⋅ JOHN ADAMS ⋅

*J*ohn Adams, *a prominent political and constitutional theorist of the Revolution, a leading advocate for independence in the Continental Congress, and eventually second president of the United States, was born in Braintree, Massachusetts on October 19, 1735. He studied law after graduating from Harvard in 1755 and rose to prominence as one of Boston's leading patriot advocates during the 1760s.*

His stature among the Massachusetts patriots remained unaffected by his successful defense of the British soldiers tried for murder in the aftermath of the Boston Massacre. However, in February 1771 he experienced a physical collapse, apparently from exhaustion. An episode of severe chest pains, possibly a mild heart attack, was followed by a pro-

longed, paralyzing depression. In an effort to break its grip, Adams set out at the end of May 1771 on a journey to the springs in Stafford, Connecticut, which had recently acquired a reputation for curative powers. After tarrying three days at Stafford he pushed on to explore the Connecticut River valley. The journey seems to have wrought the desired cure and Adams thus became one of the first refugees from urban stress to succeed in regaining a sense of himself in Connecticut's more pastoral, provincial setting.

The passage begins with Adams's arrival at Stafford.

R. B.

1771   Lodged at Colburns the first house in Stafford, there I found one David Orcutt, who came from Bridgwater 30 Years ago, a Relation of the Orcutts in Weymouth. He I find is also a great Advocate for the Spring. He was miserable many Years with Rheumatism &c., and by means of the Spring was now a comfortable Man. The Landlord came with [his] Father 30 Years ago from Roxbury. He has a farm of 200 Acres of Land, 100 under Improvement, keeps near 30 Head of neat Cattle, 3 Horses, 50 sheep, and yet offers to sell me his Place for L500 L.M.

1771. Tuesday. June 4th
Rode over to the Spring. One Childs had built a little House, within a few Yards of the Spring, and there some of the lame and infirm People keep. The Spring arises at the Foot of a Steep high Hill, between a Cluster of Rocks very near the Side of a River. The Water is very clear, limpid and transparent, the Rocks And Stones and Earth at the Bottom are tinged with a reddish yellow Colour, and so is the little Wooden Gutter that is placed at the Mouth of the Spring to carry the Water off—indeed the Water communicates that Colour, which resembles that of the Rust of Iron, to whatever Object it washes. Mrs. Child furnished me with a Glass

Reprinted by permission of the publisher from *Diary and Autobiography of John Adams*, vol.II edited by L.H. Butterfield, Cambridge, Mass.: Harvard University Press, Copyright © 1961 by the Massachusetts Historical Society.

Mugg, broken to Pieces and painted together again, and with that I drank
pretty plentifully of the Water. It has a Taste of fair Water with an Infusion
of some Preparation of steel in it, which I have taken, heretofore-Sal
Martis, somewhat like Copperas. They had built a shed over a little Reservoir
made of Wood, about 3 feet deep and into that conveyed the Water from
the Spring, and there People bath, Wash and plunge, for which Childs
has 8d. a time. I plunged in twice-but the 2d time was superfluous and
did me more hurt than good, it was very cold indeed.

Mrs. Child directed me to one Greens about half a Mile from the Spring,
as a Place to lodge at, and when I got there I found it was my old Acquaintance
John Green... [who] told me, to day, that he had lived in Woodstock 13
Years and had nothing but bad luck, all the Time. Now he was about
to try whether Change of Place would alter his fortune. I asked what
bad Luck? He said he had fail'd in Trade like a fool—and after Dinner
he [said] that the richest Men were such as had fail'd in Trade. His Uncle
John Chandler broke once, and very nigh breaking another Time. His
Uncle Tommy Green broke once. John Spooner broke once. So I dont
entirely despair.—This News I was natt att all surprized to hear, for I
thought fifteen Year ago, that Jno. Green would turn out so. He was a
boaster of his Vices—a great affecter of licentiousness—and at last got
in Love, like a fool, with a Girl, much too good for him. He says that
McClelan of Woodstock is the richest Man in that Town, by a great Run
of surprizing Luck in Trade in English, W. India Goods and Potash.

Dined at Greens, and after 2 Hours by Sun took my Horse and went
to the Spring again, and drank of the Water. Then I rode up the
Mountain, at the Foot of which this Spring ooses. The Hill is high And
the Prospect from it, extensive, but few cultivated Spots appear, the Horison
is chiefly Wilderness. The Mountain seems to be a Body of Oar, Iron
Oar, I suppose, in the Water filtrating thro that Mountain of Mineral's
imbibes its salubrious Quality. What Particles it is impregnated with,
I cant tell—But it is saturated with something. The Bottom and sides
of the Cistern are painted a deep yellow, and a plentifull Dust or flour

remains after the Water is drawn off. They say, that this yellow Sediment is the best thing for Scrophulous Humours, or any other Breakings out, Eruptions, Sores, Ulcers, Cankers, &c....

The Place where I now sit, in the Chamber in Greens House, has the Command of a great View, this is a Mountainous Country. This House stands upon very high Land, and here is a fine spacious Road laid out very wide and of Great length and quite strait, which lies right before me now, with the Meeting House in the Middle of it, more than half a Mile off.

Coll. Abijah Willard and Sam Ward and another bought of Wm. Brown of Salem, or Virginia, 7000 Acres of Land in this Town, and they are about erecting Iron Mills here, Furnaces, &c. and there is a Talk of making this a Shire Town, &c. Unimproved Land is to be bought in this Town in Great Plenty for 6s. an Acre.

At Night, Green call'd to his Wife, come put by your Work and come in, and takes his Family Bible, and reads a Chapter and then makes a long Prayer of half an Hour, and we all go to bed.

1771. Wednesday June 5th.
Rode to the Spring, drank and plunged. Dipped but once. Sky cloudy.

Activity and Industry, care, and Economy, are not the Characteristicks of this Family. Green was to set out upon a Journey to Providence to day to get Stores &c. and Stock for Trade, but he lounged and loitered away, hour after Hour till 9 O Clock before he mounted. The Cow, whose Titts strutt with Milk, is unmilked till 9 O Clock. My Horse would stand by the [Head?] Hour after Hour if I did not put him out my self, tho I call upon the father and the Sons to put him out....

About 11. O Clock arrived, Dr. McKinstry of Taunton and spoke for Lodgings for himself and Co[lborn] Barrell and his Wife.—It is not you? Is it? Says he.,—Persons in your way are subject to a certain weak Muscle and lax Fibre, which occasions Glooms to plague you. But the Spring will brace you.—I Joy and rejoice at his Arrival. I shall have Opportunity to examine him about this mineral, medicinal Water.

I have spent this day in sauntering about, down in the Pasture to
see my Horse, and over the fields in the Neighbourhood. Took my
Horse after noon and rode away East, a rugged rocky Road, to take
View of the Lands about the Town-and went to the Spring. 30
People have been there to day, they say. The Halt, the Lame, the vapoury,
hypochondriac, scrophulous, &c. all resort here. Met Dr. McKinstry
at the Spring. We mounted our Horses together, and turned away the
Western Road toward Somers to see the Improvements, that I saw
Yesterday from the Mountain by the Spring, and returned, to our
Lodgings.—The Dr. I find is a very learned Man. He said that the
Roman Empire came to its Destruction as soon as the People got set
against the Nobles and Commons as they are now in England, and
they went on Quarrelling, till one Brutus carried all before him and
enslaved em all.—Caesar, you mean Dr.—No I think it was Brutus,
want it?—Thus We see the Dr. is very Book learnt. And when we were
drinking Tea, I said, 500 Years hence there would be a great Number
of Empires in America, independent of Europe and of each other.—
Oh says he I have no Idea that the World will stand so long-not half
500 Years. The World is to conform to the Jewish Calculations, every
seventh day was to be a day of Rest, every 7TH Year was to be a Jubilee,
and the 7TH. Thousand Years will be a Thousand Years of Rest and
Jubilee-no Wars, no fightings, and there is but about 230 wanting to
compleat the 6000 Years. Till that time, there will be more furious
Warrs than ever.

Thus I find I shall have in the Dr. a fund of Entertainment. He
is superficial enough, and conceited enough, and enthusiastical enough
to entertain.

1771. Thursday June 6th.

Spent this fine day in rambling on horseback and on foot with Dr. McKinstry
East and West, North and South. Went with him twice to the Spring and
drank freely of the Waters, and rode about to hire an Horse to carry me

to Springfield and Northampton. At last obtained one. The Dr. is alert and chearfull and obliging and agreeable.

In the afternoon Colburn Barrell and his Wife and Daughter came, and took Lodgings at our House. Drank Tea and spent the Evening with them. When the Dr. took his Hat to go out to a Neighbours to lodge, Colburn sprung out of his Chair and went up to the Dr., took him by the Hand And kissed him, before all the Company in the Room. This is Sandemanianism.

Rode this day, beyond the Meeting House, and found my old Acquaintance the Parson, John Willard, at his own Door. He lives in a little, mean looking Hutt. How many of my Contemporaries at Colledge, worthy Men, live in poor and low Circumstances! Few of them have so much of this Worlds Goods as have fallen even to my Share, tho some of them have much more. Let me enjoy then what I have, and be gratefull....

1771. Fryday, June 7th.
Went to the Spring with the Dr. and drank a Glass and an half i.e. a Jill and an half. My Horse was brought very early—my own Mare I shall leave in a very fine Pasture, with Oats for her twice a Day that she may rest and recruit....

Rode to Somers, over a very high large Mountain which the People here call Chestnut Hill. It is 5 miles over, very bad Road, very high Land. It is one of a Range of great Mountains, which runs North and South Parallell with Connecticutt River, about 10 miles to the East of it, as another similar Range runs on the Western Side of it. There is a Mountain which they call the bald Mountain which you pass by as you cross Chestnutt hill, much higher from whence you can see the great River, and many of the great Turns upon it, as they say.—Dined at Kibbys, met People going over to the Spring....

Rode from Kibbys over to Enfield, which lies upon Connecticutt River, oated and drank Tea at Peases—a smart House and Landlord truly, well dressed, with his Ruffles &c., and upon Enquiry I found he was the great Man of the Town—their Representative &c. as well as Tavern Keeper, and just returned from the gen[eral] Assembly at Hartford.—Somers and Enfield are upon a Levell, a fine Champaign Country. Suffield lies over the River on the West Side of it.

Rode along the great River to Windsor, and put up at Bissalls—i.e. in East Windsor, for the Town of Windsor it seems lies on the West Side of the River.

The People in this Part of Connecticutt, make Potash, and raise a great Number of Colts, which they send to the West Indies, and barter away for Rum &c. They trade with Boston and New York but most to New York. They say there is a much greater Demand for Flaxseed of which they raise a great deal, at N. York, than there is at Boston, and they get a better Price for it. Kibby at Somers keeps a Shop, and sells W. India goods and English Trinketts, keeps a Tavern, and petty foggs it.

At Enfield you come into the great Road upon Connecticutt River, which runs back to Springfield, Deerfield, Northampton &c. Northward and down to Windsor and Hartford, Weathersfield and Middleton, Southward.

The Soil as far as I have ridden upon the River if I may judge by the Road is dry and sandy. But the Road is ¾ of a mile from the River and the intervale Land lies between.

I begin to grow weary of this idle, romantic Jaunt. I believe it would have been as well to have staid in my own Country and amused myself with my farm, and rode to Boston every day. I shall not suddenly take such a Ramble again, merely for my Health. I want to see my Wife, my Children, my Farm, my Horse, Oxen, Cows, Walls, Fences, Workmen, Office, Books, and Clerks. I want to hear the News, and the Politicks of the Day. But here I am, at Bissills in Windsor, hearing my Landlord read a Chapter in the Kitchen and go to Prayers with his Family, in the genuine Tone of a Puritan.

1771. Saturday June 8th.

Bissill says, there are Settlements, upon this River, for 300 Miles—i.e. from Seabrook [Saybrook] where it discharges itself. The River, in the Spring, when the Snow melts, swells prodigiously and brings down the Washings of Mountains and old Swamps, rotten Wood and Leaves &c. to inrich the Intervale Lands, upon its banks.

At eleven O Clock arrived at Wrights in Weathersfield. I have spent this Morning in Riding thro Paradise. My Eyes never beheld so fine a Country. From Bissills in Windsor to Hartford Ferry, 8 Miles, is one continued Street—Houses all along, and a vast Prospect of level Country on each Hand, the Lands very rich and the Husbandry pretty good. The Town of Hartford is not very compact, there are some very handsome and large Houses, some of brick. The State House is pretty large, and looks well. I stopped only to oat my Horse and get my Head and Face shaved, and then rode to Weathersfield 4 miles, on the West Side of the River.—Here is the finest Ride in America, I believe. Nothing can exceed the Beauty, and Fertility of the Country. The Lands upon the River, the flatt low Lands, are loaded with rich, noble Crops of Grass, and Grain and Corn. Wright says, some of their Lands, will yield 2 Crops of English Grass, and two Ton and an half at each Crop, and plenty of after feed besides—but these must be nicely managed and largely dunged. They have in Weathersfield a large brick Meeting House, Lockwood the Minister. A Gentleman came in and told me, that there was not such another Street in America as this at Weathersfield excepting one Hadley, and that Mr. Ingersol the Stamp Master told him, he had never seen in Phyladelphia nor in England, any Place equal to Hartford and Weathersfield.—One Joseph Webb, one Deane and one Verstille, are the principal Traders here, both in English and W. India Goods.

Dined at the Widow Griswalls [Griswolds] in Weathersfield about 3 Miles from Wrights, the Road and Country are equally pleasant all the Way. Sat down to Table with the old Woman and another Woman, and a dirty, long, greybearded Carpenter who was at Work for Landlady, and might be smelled from one Room to the other—So that these Republicans are not very decent or neat. Landlady and her Housewright very very chatty about Boston, Providence, Newport, Marthas Vineyard And Nantuckett. Landlady says the Deputy Governor calls here and always has some comical Story to tell her. He asked her tother day to come down and see his Wife make cheese. He has 22 Cows, and his Women make Cheese in the forenoon and then dress up and go out, or receive Company at home.

Rode to Middletown, and put up for the Sabbath at Shalers, near the Court House. Middleton I think is the most beautifull Town of all. When I first opened into the Town which was upon the Top of a Hill, there opened before me the most beautifull Prospect of the River, and the Intervals and Improvements, on each Side of it, and the Mountains at about 10 Miles distance both on the East and West Side of the River, and of the main Body of the Town at a Distance. I went down this Hill, and into a great Gate, which led me to the very Banks of the River. The Road lies here along the Bank of the River and on the right Hand is a fine level Tract of Interval Land as rich as the Soil of Egypt. The Lotts are divided by no Fence, but here are Strips runing back at right Angles from the River, on one is Indian Corn, on another Parrallell to it is Rye, on another Barley, on another Flax, on another a rich Burden of Clover and other English Grasses, and after riding in this enchanting Meadow for some Time you come to another Gate, which lets you into the main Body of the Town, which is ornamented as is the Meadow I just mentioned, with fine Rows of Trees and appears to me as populous, as compact and as polite as Hartford....

The Air all along from Somers to Middleton appears to me to be very clear, dry, and elastic....

In all this Ramble from Stafford, I have met with nobody that I knew, excepting Jo. Trumble, who with his father the Governor were crossing the ferry for the East Side, when I was for the West.

Bespoke Entertainment for the Sabbath, at Shalers, and drank Tea.

"Middleton I think is the most beautiful town of all." (page 35)
—John Adams

MIDDLETOWN BY M. RUSSELL. WATERCOLOR, 1799-1801. (DETAIL)

She brought me in the finest and sweetest of Wheat Bread, and Butter, as yellow as Gold, and fine Radishes, very good Tea and sugar. I regaled without Reserve. But my Wife is 150 Miles from me at least, and I am not yet homeward bound. I wish Connecticutt River flowed through Braintree. But the barren rocky Mountains of Braintree are as great a Contrast as can be conceived to the level smoth, fertile Plains of this Country. Yet Braintree pleases me more. ...

1771. Sunday, June 9th.
Feel a little discomposed this Morning. Rested but poorly last night. ...

Looking into a little bedroom, in this House Shaylers, I found a few Books, the musical Miscellany, Johnsons Dictionary, the farmers Letters, and the Ninth Volume of Dr. Clarks sermons. This last I took for my Sabbath Day Book, and read the Sermon on the Fundamentals of Christianity, which he says [are] the Doctrines concerning the Being and Providence of God, the Necessity of Repentance and Obedience to his Commands, the Certainty of a Life to come, a Resurrection from the dead and a future Judgment. ...

Went to Meeting in the Morning, and tumbled into the first Pew I could find—heard a pretty sensible, Yalensian, Connecticuttensian Preacher. At Meeting I first saw Dr. Eliot Rawson, an old School fellow. He invited me to dine. His House is handsome without, but neither clean nor elegant within, in furniture or any Thing else. His Wife is such another old Puritan as his Cousin, Peter Adams's Wife at Braintree. His Children are dirty, and ill governed. He first took me into his Physick Room, and shewed me a No. of Curiosities which he has collected in the Course of his Practice—first an odd kind of long slender Worm preserved in Spirits. He says he has had between 20 and 30 Patients with such Worms-several Yards long and some of them several Rods. He shewed me some fingers he cutt off and some Wens, and his Physick Drawers And his Machine to pound with his Pestle &c.

His dining Room is crouded with a Bed and a Cradle, &c. &c. We had a picked up Dinner. Went to Meeting with him in the Afternoon, and heard the finest Singing, that ever I heard in my Life, the front and side Galleries were crowded with Rows of Lads and Lasses, who performed all the Parts in the Utmost Perfection. I thought I was wrapped up. A Row of Women all standing up, and playing their Parts with perfect Skill and Judgment, added a Sweetness and Sprightliness to the whole which absolutely charmed me.—I saw at Meeting this Afternoon Moses Paine, who made a decent Appearance and the Dr. tells me lives by his Trade of a shoemaker comfortably from Day to day.

The more I see of this Town the more I admire it. I regrett extremely that I cant pursue my Tour to New Haven. ...

Drank Tea with Landlady, and her Son Mr. Shaylor, in pretty, western Room. But they are not very sociable. In short, I have been most miserably destitute of Conversation here. The People here all Trade to N. York, and have very little Connection with Boston. After Tea went over to the Drs., and found him very social and very learned. We talked much about History &c. He says, that Boston lost the Trade of this Colony by the severe Laws vs. their old Tenor. But they may easily regain the Trade, for the People here are much disgusted with N. York for their Defection from the N[on] Importation Agreement, and for some frauds and unfair Practises in Trade. He says they have found out that N. York Merchants have wrote home to the Manufacturers in England to make their Goods narrower and of a meaner fabric that they might sell cheaper, and undersell Boston. ...

1771. Monday June 10th.
Took my Departure from Middleton, homewards, the same Way I went down. Very hot. Oated at Hartford, and reached Bissills of Winser, 23 Miles before Dinner, just as they had got their Indian Pudding and their Pork and Greens upon the Table, one quarter after 12. After Dinner attempted to cutt off an Angle, by striking over by Goshen, i.e.

Ellington, to Kibbys at Somers, but lost my Way, and got bewildered among Woods and cross Paths, and after riding 10 Miles to no Purpose returned to Bissills, and took the old Rout to Enfield, excessive hot. Lodged at Peases. But passed a very restless uncomfortable Night. Overcome with Fatigue and inflamed with Heat I could not sleep. And my Meditations on my Pillow were unhappy.

1771. Tuesday June 11.
Rode to Kibbys at Somers but got caught in the Rain—very heavy plentifull Showers—I was much wet. Thus I have hitherto had not very good Luck upon my homeward bound Voyage. Dined at Kibbys and then rode over the Mountain to Stafford, went to the Spring and drank of the Waters with a Gentleman from New Jersey, who was there, with a Servant. Dr. McKinstry was gone to Brookfield, to accompany Mr. Barrell so far in his Way home.

1771. Wednesday June 12.
Set out upon my Return home.

REVOLUTIONARY CONNECTICUT

However primitive and provincial Connecticut may have seemed to visitors during the colonial period, the Revolution thrust all the United States, Connecticut not excluded, before the larger European world. During the Revolutionary War the state either played host to or was traversed by a substantial body of French and other non-English speaking visitors. Accordingly, one of the travel accounts in this section is by a Frenchman, another by a Yorkshire gentleman, and only two by Americans. Ironically, America was almost as alien to these Americans as it was to the Europeans. One came from a remote section of the young republic and had been educated in Europe. The other was an internal alien, radically out of sympathy with those who controlled Connecticut's political system.

Despite the widely differing perspectives behind each of the following accounts, all the passages convey the impression of Connecticut as a stable, republican society. None seem terribly interested in the Revolution through which the state was passing or had recently passed. Instead, most of the writers noted the beauty of the countryside and subscribed explicitly or implicitly to the idea that Connecticut was the land of "steady habits," a myth whose origins reached back to the colonial past. All four note the religious nature of the state's culture. Finally, all the passages but the one by Landolphe record the impressions of visitors who came to Connecticut overland. Their point of entry provided them with an additional contrast against which to measure what they encountered in Connecticut.

Generally speaking each of the observations reprinted below
assumed the state's character was more stable and fixed than it in fact
it turned out to be. That misperception flowed from a desire to construe
Connecticut as the embodiment of certain static values, either positively
or negatively. Even with the inaccuracies, misconceptions, and biases
of the following accounts, however, they provide a form of unmediated
access to the nature of revolutionary Connecticut that is available in few
other sources.

❧ JEAN-FRANCOIS LANDOLPHE ☙

*Jean-Francois Landolphe was born in 1747, one of twenty-two chil-
dren of a mercenary soldier in the employ of a French nobleman.
Landolphe worked his way up in the merchant service from ship's boy
to sailing master and during the American war assumed command of
a frigate-sized armed vessel,* La Negresse, *probably sailing under royal
charter. In October 1779 he was escorting two other vessels back from
the Caribbean to Europe when they encountered a powerful storm that
severely damaged all three ships. A chance encounter with an American
privateer led them to put into New London just as the British were evac-
uating their position at Newport. Shortly after their arrival, they were
frozen in by the extraordinarily cold winter of 1779-1780. Landolphe
managed to refit* La Negresse *by cannibalizing the other two ships that
accompanied him, but did not succeed in clearing New London until
the beginning of the following May.*

*The passage below, recording Landolphe's experiences in Connecticut
during the half-year he remained there, was written fifty years after the
fact, when the author was in his 70s. Some of the events he records, such
as the encounter with Washington, could not have happened as recorded
in this memoir. However, Landophe convincingly contrasts the warm*

welcome extended to his little fleet by most New Londoners—best exemplified by the magnanimity of the person who refused the promised reward for returning his pocketbook—with the litigiousness of the pilot who had brought them into port. In this connection, readers should bear in mind that the continental currency collapsed between October 1779 and March 1780. Landolphe's memories of the ensuing winter, though perhaps embellished over time, also appear to be authentic as does his account of the way he outfitted La Negresse *for the return journey to France. It is unlikely that John Trumbull would have sought passage to France on her had she not seemed a sound vessel of unusual strength.*

R. B.

1779   At ten in the morning we doubled the point of this island, and on the eleventh we made our entry into New London, dropping anchor there. The fort greeted us with fifteen cannon shot, a number which stands for the United Provinces. We replied to the salute with the same number of shots.

I went ashore with the captain. Together we went to pay a visit to the commander of the place and to M. Deschamps, naval officer of the port. ...

A few moments after our arrival in that city we wrote to the French consul-general informing him of our misfortune and asking him to name commissioners to assess the damage which the storm had done to the structure, masts, rigging and gear of the ships and to the merchandise. He let us know by way of reply that he was deeply sympathetic to us in our trouble, but that it was imperative for each of us to make a statement individually and in person, so that this testimony could be authenticated. In keeping with this advice we decided to make the trip to Boston.

Before we left we summoned the American pilot who had guided us in. We wanted to settle the price which he was asking for his services.

Excerpted from "A French Sea Captain in Revolutionary Connecticut: Extract from the Memoirs of J.F. Landolphe," Marcou R. Cox, from 2nd ed., *The Connecticut Historical Society Bulletin*, vol. 47, no. 2, April 1982, courtesy of The Connecticut Historical Society, Hartford.

He wanted seven hundred dollars from each captain, or seven hundred francs, because a dollar in paper money was at that time approximately equal to a franc. I was ready to pay him the sum, when my two colleagues, finding it excessively high objected to my acknowledging it, saying that if I receipted such a sum, it would become a standard price for them, and they considered it much too high for the service which the pilot had provided. I acceded to their arguments, and we decided that the amount to be paid would be determined on our return from Boston.

The day after our entry into New London, October 12, it began to feel cold. It was so severe in fact that two days later the port iced over. The townspeople warned me that the winter would be very harsh and very long; that neither I nor my crew could possibly spend it aboard the ship. This information made me rent a fine house at the dock where my vessel was moored. The sailors went ashore. Their hammocks were set up on the ground floor of this house. Since I needed money to buy provisions, cannon, and powder to equip and repair the ship once again, I announced that the remaining spoiled sugar and coffee, which I feared losing altogether if I waited longer, was for sale.

I had the foodstuffs put in a store near the docks. Soon thereafter the sale was successfully underway. Crowds of customers came and asked for the very things which had suffered the greatest damage: coffee for three dollars a pound, sugar for two—all of which brought me in a sum of twenty-four thousand francs which I put in a clasped pocket-book.

The following day, again accompanied by the captains, I went to visit General Washington, who had come from Philadelphia to have an interview with Generals LaFayette and Rochambeau. General Washington seemed to be deeply touched by our visit. He said to us: "I was really sorry to learn about setbacks which the hurricane caused you. On what day do you think you'll be leaving for Boston?" "Tommorrow, General." "You'll no doubt go on horseback?" "Yes, General." "You'll have to have an interpreter. Get in touch with the commanding officer here. He will arrange this for you."

The following morning three fine horses were brought to us, along with a very well mounted interpreter. We bedded down in Norwich, a pretty little town six leagues from New London, where we found an excellent supper as well as a very good bed. In the morning, before our departure, we were served coffee with milk and slices of bread with butter and cheese. When it came time to pay, we were met with a refusal. We looked at each other in astonishment; and since we felt it was essential to know the cause of such behavior, the interpreter, at our insistence, told us that he was under orders to make our names and ranks known in all the inns we stayed at on the way to Boston.

We then proceeded to the village of Walington, which is inhabited by a tribe of savages who have put themselves under the protection of the American government. They live in complete freedom, subject to no constraint, and have no occupation other than roebuck hunting.

Beyond this village a great quantity of snow covered the ground. When I was obliged to dismount, my pocketbook fell out of my overcoat without my noticing it. It was only in Boston that I discovered this loss. I felt it the more because it involved a number of individuals to whom the sugar and coffee which I had sold belonged. We went directly to the consul so as to set before him the statement which he had asked for. I was careful not to omit an account of the lost pocketbook and the money which it contained. My two colleges, who had been apprized of its worth when they set out, confirmed my story. We asked him to serve as our agent for any remaining business during the rest of our stay in those parts. Not only did he readily accept, but he cordially offered to provide us any services which he might personally perform. So cordial were the proceedings that I felt I could not leave him in ignorance of my latest misfortune. I therefore told him the sad story. He reassured me at once, saying: "Your pocketbook can easily be found. This colony, being newly settled, is inhabited only by people who own property. Have a notice about this accident put in the public papers. Describe all the circumstances in detail, up to and including the color of the pocketbook. Promise a big reward to whoever brings it back. Include a mention of your name, rank, and place of residence. Give me the note. I have a slight acquaintance with one of the editors of the most widely read newspapers. I will bring it to his attention." The notice was drawn up within the hour.

After staying in Boston a week to make various arrangements with the consul, we decided that he should officially name four experts who would come to New London to assess the damages done to the *Jonathon* and the *Comte d'Artois*. Their daily expenses were fixed at three dollars each. On the eve of our departure, a representative of the local commanding officer came to offer us three horses, and at eight o'clock the next morning a guide-interpreter brought them. We set out for New London which we reached on the fourth day. The experts did not get there until a week after us.

Captains André and Gireaud had their ships unloaded; each barrel of spoiled coffee and sugar was entered into an official record. We then hired carpenters who, after a scrupulous examination, condemned the two vessels to be taken out of service-the investment they required being out of proportion to their usefulness, and the extensive repairs of the ships being impossible moreover in a country which was short of resources and materials for this purpose. Such was the verdict of the experts.

Some among them held that the same verdict should apply to the *Negresse*, but I was strongly opposed; because despite the fact that heavy expenditures were required for refitting, for masts, guns, powder, munitions, and for provisions, I perceived that my sails and line were sufficient for a new rigging. I therefore resolved to fit it out in the spring—forced to submit to this delay by the rigors of a freeze which registered between thirty and thirty-five degrees on the Reaumur thermometer. The ice on the rivers was extremely thick and the sea itself was iced over to a distance of three leagues from the coast, so that ships of all kinds were unable to enter or leave the port.

I informed André and Gireaud that after the *Negresse* was repaired, I would voluntarily undertake to transport the coffee and sugar which they still had aboard to France, along with their passengers and crew. I bade them keep silent about my intentions, for fear of being spied upon by friends of the English at our departure, and, the better to mislead those latter, I spread the rumor that my plan was to head to Baltimore, where I was going to pick up a consignment of tobacco...

By now it was November, and the freeze was so deep that even the heaviest vehicles were able to cross rivers on the ice. Fortunately, an abundance of foodstuffs was still coming in. Farmers brought us their slaughtered livestock by sled, and sold it to us by the pound: hens, one dollar; fat turkeys, two; hogs, two; sheep, one and a half; beef, one. Of this last kind of meat I bought little, because M. Constant, after assuring me that the winter would indubitably be hard, advised me to acquire live cattle. I heeded this advice. I bought twenty head, ten of which were slaughtered soon thereafter for lack of fodder. The ship's butcher hung them in a huge storehouse, but within twelve hours the cold had hardened them so much that an axe was needed to pry the pieces apart. The others were slaughtered to meet our daily needs, which were considerable because, aside from the one-hundred twenty men of my crew, I still had the two captains and their officers at my table.

The cooks and bakers of the three ships saw to the sailors' common nourishment. My house had three stories. A very large stove had been installed in which I burned a cord of wood a day. It sold for so little that it cost me no more than it was worth to ship it—about twenty *sous* a cord. I put in a provision of one hundred cords, imagining that some would be left over at the time of my departure; but I made a grave error in my calculations because, at the end of January, as the cold grew more intense, I found myself compelled to build up my provision all over again, which cost me six times more. At the end, in March, a new purchase came to fifteen francs a cord.

I spent three months at leisure, aside from those pleasant times when I hunted with the savages, whose marvelous talent for this activity is well known.

By the last days of November I was dreaming sadly on the dock about the ruin of my ship. I said to myself: I have resolved to fit this ship out; if I fail in my purpose, what will people think? Won't they justifiably accuse me of imprudence? Won't I deserve the mockery which young hotheads bring down upon themselves? These reflections were suddenly interrupted by a man—elegantly dressed in grey—whom I can still see in my mind. He clapped me on the shoulder and asked in English if my name was Captain Landolphe. "Yes, that is my name and rank. What do you want of me?" "Have you lost a pocketbook?" "Yes, forty days ago." "Can you furnish proof that you are the one who incurred the loss?" "No doubt about it! That won't be hard. Ask the officers and crew from my ship. I trust that their testimony will be sufficiently convincing." "Is there a notary in this city?" "I don't know; but if you would please go with me to my correspondent, you will have the information which you seem to need." "I am willing to."

When we arrived at M. Constant's, the Englishman asked him if he knew me. "Oh, yes, very well." "In that case, let's go see a notary." "Why?" "I must make an official statement on behalf of the captain." "Agreed." Once we were at the notary's residence, the unknown man said to me: "Last October the newspapers announced that you had lost a pocketbook. Please describe this object in detail." "It is made of red morocco leather and closes with a key like this," I said, holding up my watch chain. "If you open it, you will find my name inscribed in gold letters in the inside of the cover." When my statement of verification was over, the man added, "I found it quite a long time ago. Its striking color against the snow made me notice it. I was on horseback. I got down to pick it up. I was going to Charlestown. I have traveled more than three hundred leagues since then. This explains my delay in getting it back to you."

As soon as it had passed from the notary's hands into mine, I hastened to hand over the sum of ten thousand dollars which I had promised, but this high-principled man refused. Deeply touched by his generous sentiments, I asked him if he were a sailor. When he replied in the affirmative, I begged him to take one barrel of sugar and another of coffee for his wife. I had the pleasure of seeing him accept this present as well as dinner, during which I introduced him to my two colleagues and our officers, who showed him great consideration and esteem.

Around this time so much snow fell over a three-day period that it rose above the windows of the second story, in such manner that daylight could not penetrate. I had never seen anything like it. I was told that during this season this was an ordinary occurrence in the country, and that a law obliged every inhabitant of the countryside to provide shelter for all travelers—those who traveled by horse as well as those on foot, and even carters—because when the snowfall is so thick as to shut out the light of the sky the life of these travelers is too much at risk.

To set up communications with my neighbors across the street I had a vaulted passage dug beneath the snow. Every man in New London went to great lengths to get rid of the snow. Most threw it into a pile in the middle of the street, and made hummocks with it. A path just large enough for two people abreast was left in front of every house. We were hoping that a thaw would soon melt all the snow. Alas! Our miscalculation was exceeded only by our impatience to see fair weather again. The cold set in again with an extraordinary harshness. It made us all numb. I bought some fox hides to make myself a vest, and I wore it fur side to my skin. My overcoat was lined in the same way. I wore a bearskin cap on my head. Other furs, equally warm, lined the inside of my boots. The captain and other officers copied this outfit. They found it suited them very well. The snow was soon as hard as the ice, and people moved about only in sleighs. ...

During the last days of this month I thought about getting hold of some masts, guns, and powder. In port at that time was a well fitted-out frigate, belonging to the United States, called the *Tremboule*, which was commanded by Nickelson. I went to see this captain every day. I often gave him advice for which he was grateful. One of my observations had to do with his guns.

I told him they looked too short; that in the heat of a prolonged fight they might come loose from their emplacements, and that to me it seemed prudent as well as advantageous to order one of larger dimensions. He conceded that my reasoning was sound but added that he would have to talk about it to M. Deschamps. "If," I said to him, "your cannon are condemned, I will take them aboard my ship to accommodate you, because they will serve my needs for one crossing."

We went together to the naval officer of the port and told him the purpose of our visit. Our arguments seemed convincing to him. The guns were consigned to me at the price at which they had been appraised. A new battery of longer and larger pieces was then ordered from the Boston foundry for the frigate. When an inspection by expert carpenters revealed its mainmast to be three feet too short, I requested it for my ship, the granting of which request caused me great satisfaction. Soon thereafter the mast was removed from the frigate, and without changing the proportion of the mast in any way, it was put on the *Negresse*. While waiting for the season to grow milder, I gave orders for caulking. The men got busy repairing the sails and working in the storerooms.

I had to think about provisions, I needed a lot of biscuit, salt beef, fat, and things to drink. Flour was very scarce throughout Connecticut, where I was living. The other provinces had been forbidden to ship any outside their boundaries without the consent of Congress. The naval officer of the port got me out of this difficulty by taking it upon himself to obtain in my name an authorization for importing two hundred barrels of flour, one hundred barrels of salt beef, and fifty barrels of lard from Virginia. The full amount was allocated by virtue of a simple statement on the part of the naval officer of the port, and promptly arrived. My two bakers, the ones from the *Jonathon* and the *Comte d'Artois,* and four others from the locality made biscuit. They turned out three or four hundred pounds a day.

The crew and passengers were visibly satisfied to see the success of my plans. Every evening they treated themselves to dancing and other forms of diversion. The inhabitants of New London took us out on five or six league sleigh rides, often to Norwich. The ladies, wrapped up in fine furs, footwarmers at their feet, ardently partook of this pleasure. Each sleigh held eight people and was drawn by two beautiful, bell-festooned coursers, astride which sat two nimble grooms who drove them at a fast and constant trot. We always set out at six or seven in the evening-under a lovely moon. On arrival at the place in town in which we'd been invited, we would eat and then dance through the night. At five in the morning the host would serve tea and café au lait with little cakes. One or two hours later we would set out again, and go on to New London to rest after the rigors of the trip. There were eight sleighs at a time for the parties, each of which carried four men and four ladies.

These activities proved very salutary during the cold weather, and we managed to get some hunting in as well. Since hare and partridge are very common in that locality, we bagged large quantities of these. The partridge in these parts is different from its counterpart in Europe, in that it whistles and perches in trees; aside from that the plumage is the same.

I wanted to careen my ship, but up to the last days of March, when it began to abate, the cold weather prevented me from doing this. The ice around the ship was more than five feet thick. I gave orders to have it broken up with sledge-hammers and crowbars. By dint of continuous effort this was finally done. The *Negresse* was moored to the shore, a careening apparatus was set up on the dock. We inspected the free-board, and were shocked to see a fragment of rock weighing more than sixty pounds lodged in the planking three feet from the keel. We had a lot of trouble prying it out of the wood. It was a stone from Cayes-d'Argent where I had run ashore the year before on April 30. If it had come loose at the time, we would have been lost for sure. The ship would have gone to the bottom. The opening caused by this mishap was more than eighteen inches in diameter. It was truly marvelous to see the surprise and admiration which spread over the faces of all those present at my good fortune.

The repairs went on apace. After the caulking, I had an inch-thick layer of tallow mixed with white-lead and lime-water applied to the freeboard in order to increase the speed of my ship....

My provisions were brought aboard in April. As there was very little wine, and what there was cost dear, I bought forty hogsheads of excellent cider to take its place. It was then that the rumor (which I myself had spread in the hopes that the enemy frigates cruising before the harbor would raise their stations) got about that I was going to Baltimore.

I also acquired, from a wholesale dealer in New London, four hundred hogsheads of leaf tobacco at fifteen francs a hundred weight, which I was still able to pay out of the proceeds of my spoiled sugar and coffee. I left room for the foodstuffs from the *Jonathon* and the *Comte d'Artois*, which I had promised to take aboard.

By April 20 the crew had finished bringing the victuals and guns aboard. The ship itself had been rigged to perfection, when the naval officer of the port asked me to visit him. It was to ask me if I would be willing to take on two passengers in whom he took great interest, and who wanted to see France. One was M. Tramboule [John Trumbull], an infantry major in the United States Army, and the son of the governor of the province of Connecticut. The other was named M. Laurence, major in chief in the same army, but who at this time also figured in the capacity of doctor. I have thought since then that these two personages had a secret mission from Congress to Minister Franklin.

I told the naval officer of the port that I considered myself lucky to be able to do something he wanted on behalf of these gentlemen, although the *Negresse* was already loaded down with three crews and forty passengers (because, aside from my own, I was carrying people from the other ships, which came to a total of three hundred ninety persons, among whom eleven women were to be counted. With so many brave and bellicose people aboard I felt no dread at the prospect of meeting enemy frigates of my size.

I gave the passengers notice that they should get ready to leave; for I meant to set sail at the first hint of a thaw. Assured of their passage, Messrs. Tremboule and Laurence came to see me every day. They seemed highly pleased with the size of my ship and with the quarters I was assigning them. The former, who spoke French rather well, asked if he might be allowed to draw it, so he could send a picture of it to his father, which request I granted with pleasure. He then said to me, "I know that on a long trip the French like poultry a lot. I am also aware that the passengers have to provide their own food. I have not brought any aboard on my own account, but I am going to make a special effort to put a nice chicken coop in for you here."

This offer was very timely, because I was beginning to feel some trepidation about satisfying the large number of people who were to be fed at my table. My fears were fortunately short-lived. I saw several sleighs arriving shortly-loaded with enormous cages which were stuffed (by our count) with more than three hundred hens, ducks, geese, and turkeys. Six big pigs followed the poultry. I did not have the kind of cages which were needed to hold them. The naval officer of the port provided them. I then announced to the passengers that a plumed legion was about to arrive and that a barracks was being built for them on shore. They were much amused to see this new resource for our voyage.

On the eighth of May, after Captains Gireaud and André had sent me all their goods, I went to Captain Nickelson, and informed him of my scheme for having my crew saw me out of the ice which still held me in its grip. He smiled at the unusual nature of the project, and then said to me: "You can be assured that if it succeeds, I shall set sail right afterwards. Together we shall keep to the same course one hundred leagues to the east. I shall shortly take it upon myself to draw up a table of signals which we can use in case we sight the enemy."

Back aboard, I questioned the carpenter about the number of long saws which he had available. He owned only two. I asked M. Constant to provide two others. The lower part of the four saws was detached. I had four twelve-gauge cannon balls attached to each blade. Cannon-pliers dug big holes in the ice, which was still more than fifteen inches thick. Once the tools were in place, they rapidly sawed around the ship. Once the success of my undertaking was no longer in doubt, I ordered forty of my sailors to keep it going from the harbor to the sea. Long lines were traced on the ice to guide the blades of the saw, and the cutting proceeded with incredible celerity. The sailors removed the sawed squares from the harbor with launches. The currents in the middle of the river proved surprisingly favorable to this painful work, which proceeded with a doggedness which mightily impressed the townspeople of New London—to whom the spectacle was as unusual as it was admirable. After more than six months of waiting, a passage to the sea opened before me on a single day, because the operation which began on the ninth was finished by the morrow.

The commander of the American frigate congratulated me on such a rapid success. I informed him that I would leave on the twelfth. He told me that he intended to do the same, and gave me his signals. I had the drum summon the officers and sailors aboard to receive a well-deserved recompense for their zealous work repairing my ship. As it was three in the afternoon no one missed the summons.

I ordered the second and first lieutenants to go ashore and cut us loose from our moorings, and on returning aboard to set sail so as to drop anchor near the *Tremboule*. A cannon shot-the signal for departure-was fired, serving notice on the passengers to bring their effects on board at once.

I had to have a pilot for the coast. For this purpose I turned to M. Constant who told me: "I know one who's very smart, but you'll have to pay him dear." "Price is the least of my worries. Let's go see this man." "He lives two leagues out of town. We'll go talk to him this evening."

We were on our horses at ten o'clock. We knocked at the pilot's door. He put his head to the window—not wanting to open. After listening to our reasons, however, he consented to let us in. I asked him to pilot my vessel to the head of the Nantucket Banks. This feat, in his estimation, was going to be hard to bring off, because two British frigates were cruising before New London. I promised him fifty guineas if he could keep me out of enemy hands.

"I accept," he replied, "and I swear on my head that the frigate will not be able to reach you, nor even notice you, in the straits where I'll be sailing during the night. Don't be frightened when I steer close to Black Rock. I know the narrows that lie between that shoal and the shore like the back of my hand." The money (as usual) made the difficulties which had seemed insurmountable in the beginning disappear in the twinkling of an eye.

He then came with us and was assigned to duty aboard the ship. Captain Nickelson, after congratulating me on finding the pilot, told me that he would be ready himself in the course of the day, at six in the evening. After making sure that all the sailors and passengers were on board, I weighed anchor on the twelfth, and all the sails were spread. The *Tremboule* followed close behind.

WILLIAM LOUGHTON SMITH

William Loughton Smith was born to a prominent South Carolina family in 1758. At the age of twelve he was sent to England for schooling. Admitted to study law at the Middle Temple in 1774, he chose instead to continue his studies in Geneva between 1774-1778. In 1779, after two months in Paris, he went to England where he remained until the end of the Revolutionary War. Returning to Charleston in 1783, he was promptly admitted to the bar and in 1784 elected to the South Carolina legislature. In 1785 he was appointed to the state's Privy Council and in 1788 was chosen one of the state's representatives to the first Congress where he became a strong supporter of Federal policies and of Hamilton's plan for funding the revolutionary debt.

During the autumn of 1789 Washington toured all the northern and eastern states with the exception of Rhode Island, which had refused to ratify the Constitution. After Congress's adjournment in the summer of 1790, Washington made a brief visit to Newport and Providence to acknowledge Rhode Island's recent change of heart and incorporation into the Federal Union. Smith joined the President's party which included Secretary of State Jefferson, and Governor Clinton of New York. When on August 19 Washington embarked at Providence to return to New York, Smith elected to continue a tour through Connecticut, western Massachusetts, Vermont, and New York on his own. We pick up on his account as he enters the state from Rhode Island.

R. B.

1790 Notwithstanding the roads were extremely disagreeable and fatiguing, yet the prospects were pleasant; distant hills and woods, and occasionally a rapid stream, and now and then some well-cultivated fields enlivened the scene; to this was added some very fine weather, so that my journey to Hartford was a pleasant one. I left Manchester's tavern early on Friday morning, on my way to Norwich. My landlord complained bitterly of taxes. He said he paid about fifteen pounds lawful money a year; that his farm consisted of 200 acres, one-half of which was improved, and that he could barely make a living. The land certainly required great labor, as it appeared nearly covered with stones, and the road to Providence is so bad as to render the transportation of produce very inconvenient and expensive.

I breakfasted at Nixon's tavern at Valenton, thirteen miles. My landlord here, has two smart daughters whose heads were ornamented with wigs, which are much worn by the lower class of females in New England: these wigs are convenient and give considerable smartness to the appearance when well-frizzed and powdered, and are always handy; they are hung up in the room and when any company appears they are

Excerpted from "Journal of William Loughton Smith, 1790-1791," Massachusetts Historical Society, *Proceedings*, 51 (1918).

fixed on the head in a moment. From Valenton I passed through Plainfield, a pretty country town. From a high hill which I ascended there is a very magnificent prospect of an extensive range of country, some miles around Plainfield-a highly cultivated plain interspersed with woods and surrounded by beautiful hills, illuminated by a bright sun, opened a charming view just as I reached the brow of the hill, and struck me with an agreeable surprise. A similar view appeared just as I arrived within a mile or two of Norwich, which is a very neat town with several handsome houses. I dined at Norwich, and after dinner paid a visit to Mr. B. Huntingdon, a member of the House of Representatives in Congress. He has a large family, and his eldest son is a coachmaker. He accompanied me in a walk; we ascended a high rocky hill, which divided Norwich into two parts, called Up-town and Down-town, which distinctions have created distinctions among the inhabitants. The Up-town part is called sometimes "Bean Hill," arising from a report which the inhabitants had spread by way of derision, that the Up-town people had a way of eating beans and bacon every Saturday for supper. This report introduced the custom in both parts of the Town, and the inhabitants now regularly sup on Saturday on beans and bacon. From the hill (where the Meeting house formerly stood) is a charming prospect: the Town is extensive and spread before the traveler surrounded by a well-cultivated and thickly settled country; Norwich landing is about two miles distant. After I had paid a visit to the Governor, Samuel Huntingdon, formerly President of Congress, I hired a chaise and rode ten miles that evening, to Mr. Jona. Trumbull's at Lebanon; the road was rather rough but the country was picturesque. About Norwich there are several romantic scenes, a river, woods, and high hills diversify the prospect every moment. Lebanon is a valuable township, the lands fertile and well-cultivated: they export their produce to Norwich landing, from whence there is good navigation fourteen miles to New London. Mr. B. Huntingdon, the member of Congress, attended me at the inn till I set off from Norwich. I had directed the landlord (Mr. Brown, a very civil man who keeps a good house) to hire me a one horse chaise; it was brought to the door while Mr. Huntingdon was with me, who knew that I had hired it from my landlord. A little boy accompanied me as agreed, to bring the chaise back; on the road I asked him whose horse and chaise it was, and was greatly surprised to find that it belonged to my friend Mr. B. Huntingdon, of whom my landlord had hired them; he has a large family and this is one of his resources to get money.

I past the night at my acquaintance Trumbull's; he has a farm of 200 acres, reckoned a very considerable one, and lives comfortably on it. The next morning the stage called on me and we reached Hartford at four o'clock in the afternoon. The road from Norwich to Hartford is less stony and disagreeable than that from Providence to Norwich, but is far from being smooth or pleasant to travel over in a carriage; one is, however, indemnified by a succession of pleasing views. The whole way from Norwich the country is thickly settled, farm houses in sight constantly, the country well-cultivated, meadows, hills, and distant woods rising one above the other. We passed through several towns. I stopped at one about nineteen miles from Norwich, and took a view of the church-yard; from the age of many of the deceased the climate must be very healthy. The inhabitants did not, however, shine in the poetical line, to judge at least from the versification on the tombstones, a specimen of which is in these words:

> Behold as you pass by
> As you are now, so once was I;
> As I am now, so you must be,
> Prepare for death and follow me.

On the tomb-stone of Deborah House, a great name in this Town, was written "She lived desirable, and died lamented." I dined at Woodbridge's tavern, nine miles from Hartford. The road from this place, which is called East Hartford, is smooth and good; a few miles before I arrived at the river, I had from an eminence as I crossed the Bolton hills, an extensive view of a fine country, and caught a distant glimpse of Connecticut Towns. There is also a most charming view a mile or two after leaving the tavern, of a rich plain containing meadows and woods.

At Hartford I crossed the ferry over the Connecticut River, which is navigable up to this place for large sloops. About sixty sea vessels belong to Hartford, which carries on much business and is a flourishing town. The river frequently changes its bed, and by its deviations occasions much alteration of property, and gives rise to many law suits, a circumstance not disagreeable to the people of Connecticut, who are acknowledged by themselves to be very litigious; this spirit they account for from their being so well-informed, their knowledge of their rights and their equality makes them extremely jealous of any encroachment or invasion and they are determined rather to incur the expense of law (which is cheap enough) than to risk any violation of their just rights. At Hartford I saw a remarkable old oak in which the Charter of Connecticut was concealed in the year 1684 by a Mr. Wadsworth, an ancestor of the present Jeremiah Wadsworth, a member of Congress from this State. The Charter of Massachusetts had been taken away and the Governor of Connecticut was instructed to take away that of Connecticut; as it lay on the table Wadsworth blew out the candle and ran and hid this charter in a hollow part of this oak, where the Governor was unable to find it; the revolution soon after took place, and the Charter was out of danger. There is in this town an old gentleman of the name of Willis; he is upwards of eighty years of age, is the Secretary of the State, and has held that office upwards of sixty years; he is still in the full possession of his faculties and of the esteem of his countrymen, he owns a very considerable landed estate about Hartford. I had seen at Providence a Mr. Ward, upwards of forty years, which was thought a very remarkable instance of continuance in office, but that of Mr. Willis is the most extraordinary ever known. These instances and many others, are proofs of good sense in the East. Inhabitants who continue their old servants in office, as long as they behave well.

The country around Hartford is well-cultivated and the soil fertile; this is the oldest settlement in Connecticut and is perhaps the most thickly peopled part of the United States. In the towns of Connecticut I was struck with the calm and tranquility which prevails; though they are full of inhabitants, yet none are scarce seen in the streets, no carriages are moving about, and a stranger would suppose he had entered a deserted village. Here is no idleness, no lounging and chattering in the streets; every one is at work either in the field or in his house; no vagrants, no beggars to be seen; on the week-days all are at work, and on Sundays all are at home, reading the Bible. It is reckoned improper to walk about the streets and visit on Sundays; after services they all go home. Sunday forenoon I went with Col. Jeremiah Wadsworth's family to church, where I heard very good singing in parts by men and women, who stand in opposite galleries while they sing: I also heard a pretty good preacher, Mr. Strong. There are in Hartford two Meeting houses for Congregationalists and none for Episcopalians, who are very few in number. Monday morning I rode to Middletown, fifteen miles, and dined at Bigelow's tavern, and returned in the afternoon to Hartford. This was the most delightful ride I ever remembered to have taken, more beautiful scenery in that distance than in any part of my travels; the whole a most romantic country, thickly settled, highly cultivated, and adorned both by nature and art. Weathersfield about four miles from Hartford is a pretty town on the road to Middletown. After I had dined at Middletown, I rode up a hill back of the Town from which I had a most enchanting scene; looking down I saw a pretty town on the borders of a fine navigable river, a country richly cultivated, intermixed with houses and woods, the opposite banks of the river equally cultivated and bounded by rising hills, some covered with woods, others with meadows and corn fields. Returning to Hartford I enjoyed the whole way a succession of delightful prospects; first, the road for a few miles was close along the river, on one side meadows ornamented with hay-stacks and distant high hills, on the other a river ornamented with vessels sailing about and the other side romantic. Then ascending a steep hill the prospect as you turn back is extremely grand; the distant view of Middletown, a long range of the river, various hills, woods, fields, meadows, numberless settlements, and the whole bounded by lofty hills rising in masses and presenting variegated shapes. Approaching Weathersfield, another very fine scene suddenly opened from the brow of a hill over which the road runs; and extensive plain, through which the river is seen meandering, presenting the appearance of a large garden, and so thickly settled with houses that it appears like one town, the steeple of Weathersfield rising in the middle of it, the richness of verdure forms a delicious view.

Weathersfield is famous for onions, the smell of which salutes the nose of the traveller on entering the Town. Here I was shown the son of the celebrated Elizabeth Canning and the house where she lived. He is a lad about twelve or fourteen. She was brought out from England by a Mr. Williams, who settled at Weathersfield and married her to a Mr. Treat by whom she had several children; he was a respectable citizen and she was also respected by her neighbors; they are both dead. Colonel Wadsworth met me a mile beyond the Town and we ascended the steeple of Weathersfield to enjoy the view, which well rewarded us for our trouble; it is extensive, embraces Hartford and the country beyond it and surpasses all description. Tuesday a party was made on my account by Col. Wadsworth to the mountains west of Hartford. We set off after breakfast a party of about a dozen, and rode seven or eight miles to the foot of the mountain, we ascended some time a rugged, steep road; from the summit is a commanding view of a level, well-cultivated country on each side the river, with Hartford, Weathersfield, and Suffield. From the other side of the mountain, looking west, is a very grand view. Just under our feet was an immense thick forest, the top of which resembled the waves of the ocean, and appeared a considerable distance below us; a very extensive range of country lay before us to the right and left, the whole highly cultivated and interspersed with settlements; the town of Farmington is seen at a distance and the whole is extremely picturesque. At the top of the mountain is a curious pond surrounded with rocks and woods, in a very romantic situation. Upon my observing that the piece of water was disgraced by calling it a pond, and that it well merited the name of lake, it was resolved by the company that it should in future be denominated a lake, and as I was the first person who had dignified it with that appellation, it should be termed thereafter Lake Smith. We sat down to a rustic dinner (which we had carried with us) on the verdant moss in a beautiful spot, encircled with rocks and groves, with the lake just below us. In the afternoon we returned to Hartford, and I was made acquainted with Mr. John Trumbull, the celebrated author of the poem "McFingal," who supped with us at Col. Wadsworth's.

Wednesday morning we set off for Springfield; I breakfasted with Mr. Ellsworth, member of the Federal Senate from Connecticut, at Windsor, ten miles from Hartford, where he has a comfortable, neat house on a pleasant little farm. I then passed through Suffield, a pretty little town situated on an eminence and commanding a pleasing and extensive view; the Meeting house is at a little distance a fine object, being situated on very high ground. Passing on to Springfield, I crossed the Connecticut River which is wide here, and then entered the Town, which is a pretty considerable one.

ം WILLIAM STRICKLAND ം

*W*illiam Strickland was born in 1753, the eldest son of a Yorkshire baronet. As a gentleman with expectations of inheriting the principal share of his father's property, Strickland set off in July 1794, at the age of 41, to explore the United States. He took passage for America on a New England vessel to avail himself of the protection of its neutral flag while Britain was at war with France. After tarrying in New York for a month, he set off up the Hudson Valley, vis-

iting among other places the battlefield at Saratoga. On his return journey he turned east into Massachusetts, proceeding to Northampton and Springfield. From there he decided to make a detour to Hartford.

Strickland brought the sensibility of an English provincial gentleman to his encounter with the young republic. He came equipped with letters of introduction that gave him access to the Republic's gentry leadership. Just before entering Connecticut, he encountered John Adams, then the vice-president of the United States, on his way from Boston to Philadelphia, to whom he introduced himself. In Connecticut he waited on Jeremiah Wadsworth, then a member of the House of Representatives for Connecticut, and through him struck up an acquaintance with the state's governor, Samuel Huntington. Strickland was content to view the state as its leaders did. The excerpt begins as he leaves Windsor for Hartford early on a November sabbath morning.

R. B.

Sunday, November 2nd

1794   As it is not the custom in the state of Connecticut to travel on the sabbath, and contrary to the Law of it, in order to avoid giving offence, or making myself liable to be stopped, I set out as early as I could in the morning intending to spend the day at Hartford, distant about seven miles, and arrived there before 9 oClock; through a country better than that in yesterdays journey, bearing in many places a most excellent verdure, and capable of as good in every other part were it only better drained, the soil a sandy loam, in some places approaching to absolute sand, and every where, I apprehend upon a clay bottom at no great depth. Persons desirous of traveling on the Sabbath usually apply to a magistrate for a certificate, certifying the necessity of the Journey. To this the Constables, and Selectmen usually without hesitation pay respect, by

Excerpted from William Strickland, "Journal of a Tour in the United States of America, 1794-1795," ed. J.E. Strickland, *Collection of The New-York Historical Society*, vol. 83 (1971), courtesy of the New-York Historical Society.

allowing the bearer to pass, though such a certificate will not dispence with the Law. The custom however of stopping people is fast wearing out, the Law becoming obsolete; it is never put in force here, and now only in some few retired places, out of the usual line of intercourse. Some people got certificates this morning from the tavern keeper, at whose house I put up, who is a magistrate of the place.

After breakfasting with a large party, who like myself were detained here by the sanctity of the day, I waited upon Mr: [Jeremiah] Wadsworth one of the Representatives in Congress for this state to whom I had several letters of introduction, our interview at this time was short as he was preparing to attend his family to church, but he engaged me to accompany him after the service was concluded in making a tour about the vicinity of Hartford in his whiskey. The first point we made was Rockey-Hill two miles from the town. This station commands an extensive view of a rich and highly diversified country in every direction and to a considerable distance and of the beautiful vale, through which the Connecticut flows, coverd with shipping of various descriptions, this being the head of navigation for large vessels. A country as well cloathed, with as beautifully waving and wooded an outline as ever was seen, is here more thickly settled with the neat mansions of comfort and independence than the most boasted spot in our own Island; Richmond [in Surrey] with its gorgeous view, its costly palaces, cannot boast a scene like this, for there, these are contrasted and disgraced with the miserable dens of wretchedness and want, there poverty divides the multitude from the rich; ignorance from the informed, here wealth and want are equally rare and ignorance is unknown; here six schools, visible from this spot within the distance of half as many miles enlighten the mind of the child, and train him up in the way he should go, here numerous places of worship the only ostentatious buildings in view, preserve the parent in the paths of order and morality. On this rock are founded the boasted morals, the enlightened policy of the N: England States, on their virtues rest the character, the fate of America, and their virtues originate in the universal knowledge and education of the people. Here, I may confidently assert, that Englishmen may be contemplated in their greatest, most exalted character; these are now what their ancestors were, what their descendants ought to be, Alas! are not.

From this hill the meanders of this noble [Connecticut] river may be traced for many miles upwards and downwards, the towns of Weathersfield, Glastonbury, and Middletown, below Hartford, East Hartford, on the opposite banks of the river and Windsor above it are distinctly seen, and a country finely cultivated, of luxuriant verdure and richly wooded is commanded in every direction and about 15 churches with spire steeples, (the exact number I have lost) are included within the view.

From Rocky-Hill we proceeded to Weathersfield which formed a principal feature in the view from it. This is one of the neatest towns I have seen since I enterd the New-England States where all the towns are neat: it consists of many good houses detached from each other, or scatterd along a wide street, or rather along the edge of a Green of excellent turf, on a sandy soil keeping itself continually dry and firm; In the middle of this area, not half a mile asunder are three public schools, neat plain wooden buildings erected and maintained at the public expence, establishments of which nature are to be met with at certain stated distances in every part of these States.

Weathersfield is remarkable for the growth of onions, which are dispersed over every part of the U.S., and frequently sent to Europe. They grow in such luxuriance here and require such little cultivation; that the London market could be supplied cheaper with them from hence, than its own neighbourhood. The cultivators here have a peculiar method of producing early onions, worth noticing. Small ones from the size of an hazle nut, to that of a wallnut, are preserved in cellars during winter, and as early in the spring as the weather will permit, after having their old tops twisted off, are planted in favourable situations, where they soon strike root, put out fresh tops, and are sold for onions the produce of that year, but actually preceed the growth of the season by many weeks (This hint may be applied to other plants).

After returning from this pleasant excursion, I rejoined the party, but increased in number, with whom I had breakfasted, and sat down to as good a dinner, and of as various dishes and as well dressed, as a principal Inn on a great road in England would have afforded, indeed no man need wish for better entertainment than he will meet with at Frederick Bull's in Hartford. The company consisted of people from various parts of the country, and some of the town or neighbourhood, and as frequent in this country at the public tables, of the Landlord sitting at the head to carve the top dish; the conversation was easy and unrestrained but orderly, the party good humourd, communicative, and civil, and eager as I have elsewhere found such parties of conversing with a *Gentleman from the Old country*, enquiring many particulars concerning it, and frequently expressing in strong terms their attachment to the country of their forefathers; and I could not but observe here, as I have frequently done in this country before, the common practice when speaking of England of calling it *home*, the usual appellation before the revolution, but in which that great event seems hitherto to have made little alteration; dinner being over, the company speedily began to separate, and in a short time few were left, it not being the custom among an abstemious people to consume much time at the table, particularly at public tables, except a few may remain for the purpose of conversation.

In the evening I accompanyed Mr: Wadsworth to wait upon the Governour of the State, Mr: [Samuel] Huntingdon who happened to be here on public business. He has been Governour many years having been first chosen in 1785 and annually re-chosen since that period. He is usually called the Farmer Governour, being not much exalted above that rank of life. He is a respectable looking man grown gray in the service of his country, of strong sense in his conversation, of a countenance sedate, thoughtful and benignant, and of plain unaffected manners; his dress was an old fashioned black suit with ruffles reaching down to his fingers. We found him attended by two of his counsel, with whom he probably was in consultation respecting the affairs of his State. He entertained us with Cyder, wine, and apples, and while he peeled one of the last, he spread his colord India silk, handkerchief upon his knees to save his cloaths, and from thence threw the parings into the fire. The conversation during our interview, which lasted about an hour, was chiefly on general subjects, but when on that of Great Britain, here as every where else that I have had an opportunity of observing in these States, was strongly expressive of the wish of the people to keep well with it and abhorring the proceedings of those, who from the worst of motives were endeavouring to produce a rupture between the two countries.

When the Governour travels to attend the sittings of the assembly, I am told that he bestrides a pair of saddlebags, unattended by a servant; but he is every where known where he passes, and every where accompanied with the blessings of the people; such a governor requires no guard; he is not a wolf about to devour his flock, but a shepherd attending to their welfare; How great is the contrast between this Governor, and those of some other, and more distinguished countries! When compared with them, how much greater is he!

To Hartford 7 miles, expences there 21/.

The day bright and fine with a brisk N:W: wind.

Monday, November 3rd

The morning cloudy and mild with a gentle wind from S:E:.

After breakfasting with Mr: Wadsworth, was accompanyed by him to see the wollen manufactory carried on here; the establishment of this manufactory was encouraged by the Legislature of this state, which lent 9300 Dolls to sett it agoing, and aid the Company in carrying it on, and the objects of it are rather of a public than private nature. The people of Connecticut are chiefly cloathed in woollen cloths manufactured in their respective families. These for want of skill in the different operations of dying and dressing, and of mills and machinery for the purpose, were of a much inferior quality, to what they might have been; To remedy this inconvenience it was thought necessary to establish a manufactory in which workmen might receive instruction, who were afterwards to be dispersed about the country; and this accordingly was placed under the direction of a Company who in addition to what they have obtained of the state employ in it a capital of their own in return for which they are gainers in accomplishing their principal object, without at least being losers in a pecuniary view; they have already dispersed many of their apprentices about the country, and assisted them in erecting warp mills and dyaries in various places, so that these are now getting fully established. They make broad and narrow cloth, and Kerseymeres of very good quality, which though not so fine, are, I believe intrinsically better than what they get from England because made of better materials. What I saw rather resembled French than English cloth, being coarse in the thread and open in the texture, but extremely soft and pleasant in the feel, owing to the very fine wool of which it was made; the workmen employed here were chiefly English and from the West of England....

Mr: Wadsworth is extremely careful of his woodlands, being sensible that they are the most valuable part of his property, and buys as much land in this state as he is able; he bought some woodland eight yrs: since for 20 Dolls: an acre, and he has some time since been offerd 40 Dolls an acre for the timber alone which is upon it, but did not think that sum equal to the value of it; he finds timber, and wood for fuel doubled within the last ten years; wood for burning is now 20/ a cord, of 8 feet long, 4 broad, and 4 high. If care be not taken, it will soon be very scarce in this country, unless coalmines be discoverd and worked....

Mr: Wadsworth spoke very earnestly on the payment of British debts, a subject of late much agitated in all parts of the Union. Much to the honour of the New-England states nothing is due from them; his own relations paid every thing immediately after the peace was concluded, and he declared he had rather see his Son a bankrupt, than rich at the expence of his honor, and his British creditors; any man in this state who held other sentiments, would not be admitted into Society; but there is no such person in it; he reprobated in the strongest terms the dishonest proceedings of the leading characters in the Southern States, who to avoid the payment of their debts would involve their country in a war with Great Britain; this he asserted to be the Secret springs of their democracy; and for holding opposite principles, the cause of these States being accused of Aristocracy; but we are true republicans, too wise to be mislead by names, too honest to make a figure at the expence of our creditors too good politicians to desert established principles, or follow the fancies of the day. The Southern States will never move us. With these honourable sentiments I parted with my intelligent, communicative, and respectable acquaintance, each of us promising, and I believe, sincerely wishing to meet the other frequently during the winter in Philadelphia, Mr: W: being a representative of this State in Congress.

In the afternoon I set out on my journey to Boston, but not chusing to trace back my steps to Springfield, which I must have done had I taken the usual post road; and wishing to see as much of the country and manners of the people as possible, where the least affected by the intercourse of travellers, I took a little frequented road through the interior part of the country, but which in point of distance was full as short a line to Boston as the other road. I crossed the river to East-Hartford, a pretty village lying opposite to the capital of the State, and travelled through a pleasant country, but without any peculiar features to a poor tavern in Coventry township, where I was compelled to take up a nights lodging sooner than I otherwise should have done, in consequence of the evening proving very rainey.

About half way on the road, are some Glass Houses, apparently not calculated for executing much business, and chiefly employd, as I was told in making bottles, and some other ordinary articles; The weather being so bad, I could not stop to make farther enquiries concerning them....

Tuesday, November 4th

Proceed in the morning to Clark's Tavern in Coventry to breakfast. In this township a sufficient quantity of wheat to supply the inhabitants, is not grown, it is so greatly destroyed by the fly; This fly is said to be visible at this time of the Year, but no one could point it out to me....

Wednesday, November 5th

... In all the New England States education is enforced universally, as a fundamental principle of the Government; Schools are established at stated distances throughout the country, to which libraries are annexed for the use of the neighbourhood. Many of these schools I have passed on the road, and all appear numerously attended by young people of both sexes. It is found by experience here that education and knowledge promote the best interests of the Country; they do not lessen the enterprising spirit, or activity of the higher orders, for a more enterprising, and active-minded people do not exist, nor do they infringe upon the industry of the lower orders, for these last knowing the necessity of industry and labour, apply to them without repining; and all knowing the value of order and good government, and being able to appreciate the merits of their governours and government, are attached to them from principle and support them to the utmost of their power, and sensible that a government cannot prosper without order and good manners, are themselves orderly and moral. How different these from the principles held and acted upon in Europe, where many of the governments succeed in stultifying the people, and brutalizing their minds, for the purpose as they pretend of being enabled to govern them, without which they say the people would be neither industrious or be capable of being governed, but in truth, least the people should discover the demerits of their governours, and knowing them should resist and correct their abuses; and indeed where the best of the Governments do not act upon the enlightened principles of these people, not wishing to enable the people to judge of their merits, and thereby ensure their rational and willing support.

The country from Hartford to Dudley is of singular uniformity, considering the distance is so great, being every where hilly, but no where broken or mountanous, sufficiently irregular to be beautiful, without being at the same time difficult to pass; the surface is every where stony, and the soil which is heavy and retentive of water, has a principal tendency to clay. This country in general is badly cultivated, chiefly lying in rough pastures in the same state as when the timber was originally cut off, full of holes and irregularites never having been plowed. Fields are frequently to be met with which have been *laid bye* after a crop of mays, which leaves them coverd as it were with innumerable anthills, the mays being planted on hillocks made by crop plowing, about a yard asunder; such fields experience most of the pernicious consequences of such hills; this is perhaps the worst species of neglect. The natural produce of this country is black and white oak, chestnut, and Hickories of several kinds, always indicating strong and good soil, these last bearing this year and now having upon them, the greatest possible quantity of fruit; as many nuts as there have been leaves....

⊸ ELBRIDGE GERRY, JR. ⊷

Elbridge Gerry, Jr. was the son of a prominent Massachusetts politician who had been a member of the Philadelphia Convention in 1787. Though the elder Gerry had refused to sign the Constituition and opposed ratification of the document in its unamended form, he subsequently played a key role in diffusing war tensions with France in 1798-1799. On returning to the United States he became a leader of the Republican opposition in the Federalist stronghold of New England. Eventually he was elected governor of Massachusetts in 1810-11, and after losing a bitter battle against Federalist opponents in 1812 served as vice-president of the United States during Madison's second term.

His son's account of a journey taken in May 1813 through Connecticut is included in this anthology for two reasons. His is the only account of traveling from Hartford to Danbury via Farmington, Bristol, Woodbury and Newtown, a route seldom taken by those passing through the state. And he brought to his journey a strongly critical perspective derived from the Republicanism he shared with his distinguished father. New England Republicans regarded Connecticut as the stronghold of Federalism. The year before, the Republicans, under Madison's leadership, had undertaken a war against Britain to vindicate the republic and insure that the next generation would not become Federalists. The Federalist leadership of Connecticut was doing all it could to obstruct the war effort and the young Gerry thus had reason to be predisposed against what he saw of the state.

The account picks up as Gerry enters Connecticut from Sturbridge, Massachusetts.

R.B.

1813
Monday, May 3rd—I commenced a journey (southwesterly) for the benefit of my health. This I determined to perform on horseback....

May 5th

This morning being cloudy, we set off from Charlton and breakfasted at Sterbridge, and shall rest tonight at Stafford Springs where we now are. These towns, excepting Holland are the only towns we have passed through. On leaving Sterbridge you ascend a very long hill, the summit of which presents to view an extensive prospect. Situated in the centre of a circle, the prospect is bounded by hills at a greater distance than at first is supposed. This is a neat little town, and the adjacent fields are much less rocky than those we have passed by. Holland,

Excerpted from, *The Diary of Elbridge Gerry, Jr.,,* (ed. Claude G. Bowers), New York, Breatano's, 1927.

the next town, is very barren. Stafford as yet partakes of its nature; but is greatly improved in appearance by the Spring Hotel. This is situated at the foot of a high hill, on a small rising. In front a rivulet is seen to flow; and at a short distance joins two other streams. Within this rivulet is an oval yard, surrounded with a neat white fence. The house is large and very accommodating, probably can board seventy persons. Near the building are baths, cold and warm, the latter of which I shall presently refresh myself in. In a wood by the house, is a pleasant recess, presenting a natural curiosity in a rock rent by some convulsion of the earth; as I shall meet with many such I shall not at present describe it. No incident worthy of mention happened this day. My horse appears to improve and has forgot to trip often. His companion has mended greatly and will in another day travel finely. The spring water tonic is very pleasant, and has a mild and iron taste as far as I can judge. I am now going to bathe and shall close for the day.

May 6th

This morning we were aroused at 5-½, our usual hour, and were disappointed with the sound of rain against the windows. Having continued thro' the day, we have been compelled to consider Stafford as our home. To me, the day has been very agreeable within doors. There are various amusements in the house, which expel the gloomy tho't! We have a pleasant companion with us here, who is a member of New Haven College. His company has enlivened our time, and pleased us much. A week spent here is not lost by any means. My chief occupation had been in perusing Rokeby, a poem written by W. Scott, which is an agreeable companion. Last eve I tried the warm bath, and I conceive it to be the greatest luxury to the weary traveller. I have drunk copiously of the Spring Water; it is an excellent cure for indigestion, general debility, scrofulous complaints, dropsies and other disorders. For hectic complaints it is injurious.

"Stafford...is greatly improved by the appearance of the Spring Hotel." (page 73)
　　　　　　　　　　　　　　　　　　　—Elbridge Gerry, Jr.

N. WESTERN VIEW OF THE HOTEL...BELONGING TO DR. S. WILLARD AT THE MINERAL SPRINGS, IN STAFFORD, CON., BY ABNER REED. AQUATINT, 1810. (DETAIL)

May 7th

This morn we set off from Stafford and passed thro' Hamilton, Holland, Vernon, East Hartford and arrived at Hartford. We set out in a drizzly rain and very soon after it increased to a violent storm. The great change in the scene compensated for the rain in some measure. As far as Hamilton, our route lay through a country, covered with rocks; in descending a hill, all at once a most beautiful view is presented, and your sight, almost dim with efforts made in vain, is relieved by the opening. From this time the fields become green. The soil appears to be very rich and well cultivated. Holland is a small village, it is situated low and affords nothing worthy of description. Vernon is not much better. From thence to East Hartford the ride is agreeable. The entrance of this town, presents a long street divided in two by elm trees. This street continues thro' the town and is two miles in length. Around this place, the fields were clothed in verdure, the trees in full bloom, and all was cheering and enlivening to the weary traveller. We at last arrived alive at Hartford. The whole journey of today was performed in a driving storm, and hope with the blossoms of the trees encouraged us to proceed. While buffetting the rain my greatest comfort arose from anticipating a warm fire and a leisure evening; which I had already planned for writing. When thrusting my hand into my saddle bags, my heart was chilled with the feeling of wet cloths. After I paused for a moment, I began to take them out, and to my utmost horror found everything well drenched with raindrops. My next enquiry was, how to put things to rights. All my clothes were to be washed, and medicine assorted and dried, for they were chaffed into one common mixture and every article must be clothed anew. Thus were my hopes disappointed and my task assigned. This I considered as a traveler's lot and therefore to it I went. By patience and perseverance I finished by 11 at night. Thus rested, after braving a strong east wind all day with an umbrella, I retired. Hartford is a large and beautiful town. You enter it, by crossing the elegant and far famed Connecticut River. The harbour is well filled with shipping and commands the attention of the spectator on approaching the town. Hartford is regularly planned and has a state house and a number of ornamental public and private buildings. Our horses this day performed extremely well, and both have left behind their old tricks, stopping and stumbling. My horse was near being injured by a nail perforating the hind part of the saddle. But being discovered on time was remedied.

May the 8th

Having had six hours of sleep, I aroused from my slumbers and warned to prepare for another drenching. The restless impetuosity of my companion, again urged me to the unpleasant task. The day's ride preceding had convinced me that the flitting raindrops meandering down your back did not conduce much to health, or at least to comfort. After having paid dearly for my wash woman and refitted my saddle bags, I set off with the picture of my approaching condition full in my eyes. We passed thro' West Hartford, a small town, and breakfasted on a sham meal at Farmington. Here I determined to guard my baggage from the danger with which it was already threatened. I succeeded in having an oil cloth case made for it; much satisfied with the hopes of baffling the attempt of the weather, I again resumed my umbrella and position. We had now to travel ten miles to reach a tavern. As soon as we had well commenced, the storm set in and was the most violent I ever experienced. However, I trusted to my oil-case and umbrella for safety. Our road, filled with stones projecting far above the surface, was as winding as the path of a mule.... Thus situated we stemmed the torrent of adversity and arrived at Bristol. On my arrival, removing my case and holding it to the light to praise and admire it, I was struck almost blind with the innumerable holes and rents with which it was filled. My favorite case was entirely worn out, and I was compelled to cast it for a pattern. This was a trifle as I found myself in a worse plight than I was at Hartford. But the same storm that wet me gave me an afternoon to dry. I have refitted and am ready for another action. To my great joy my bold companion was thoroughly beaten by the rain and begins to adopt my future determination, never to travel in a storm. Here we are in the centre of Connecticut, whose inhabitants are bigoted and strict in their tenets. We intend to endeavour to proceed on our journey tomorrow, being Sunday; the law prohibits travelling in that day, but nothing less than death or a storm shall confine us in this state. Our journey has been entirely on turnpikes, and will continue so to the North River. Our only prayer is for fair weather and no interruptions in our next ride.

May 9th

There being a stated fine fixed to persons travelling on the Lord's day in this state, we thot it most prudent to wait untill the people were collected in meeting. We accordingly departed from Bristol, in fair weather, at that hour. We had six miles to ride, before we came to a meeting house, where the fines are in general imposed. This we soon reached and imagined every man to be a warden. By chance the storm had mitigated their vigour and we were permitted to proceed unmolested. At the next town, we had the felicity of seeing the congregation disperse, without having been members ourselves. We had now passed thro' Plymouth and Watertown. We next rode to Woodbury which terminated our day's ride...

The road passed through a barren and mountainous country; the houses were falling to pieces, and the barns tumbling to the ground. The heads of the inhabitants seem thro' holes in the houses assured us alone, that they were inhabited. Plymouth is thinly settled, but has more habitable houses. It is situated on a hill and the grounds appear less rocky and barren. Beyond this town, we travelled over part of the Green Mountains of Vermont. In ascending them, the road winded round the foot and was truly romantic. On one side a clift of rocks, almost perpendicular was seen, whose summit was scarcely reached by the tall oak. Turning from this rough and rugged side to the other, a murmuring river, gliding gently on, was nearby under your feet. Leaving this scene behind we quickly found ourselves in a basin formed by the surrounding hills. This is a curiosity; an entire circle of high hills enclose you on all sides, whose circumference is not greater than a mile. Adjoining to Plymouth is Watertown. It is at the foot of a hill on an eminence. The houses are few and handsome; the soil far better, than that of the latter town. After we had left this place, a shower came on and gave us just time to prepare for it. This rain I prevented wetting my bags, my covering with the flap of my sourtout. The shower was hardly finished, when in ascending a steep hill, a beautiful country was opened to our view. The prospect was bounded by a range of small mountains, whose sides were divided into fields, well cultivated. The whole valley was covered with verdure and ornamented with trees. In this valley the town of Woodbury was situated. It is quite a respectable village, and appears to be wealthy. There are many large houses and the country around is beautiful. As in the two former towns, there are two meeting houses close to each other, the one Episcopal, the other Congregationalist. My horse's back is worse than it was and it will be necessary to have the saddle prepared so as to avoid further injury.

May 10th

After being well entertained and attentively treated by our landlord, Mr. Hatch, we left Woodbury early this morn, and went thro' Southbury, Newtown, and shall rest at Danbury. Our ride in the morning was peculiarly agreeable. After travelling some days in the worst of weather, we were escorted out of town by various kinds of birds, saluting us continually with their cheerful notes. The remaining part of the journey was thro' a country similar to yesterday's. Mounting immense hills, they afforded a prospect almost unbounded. The country has not been so fertile, as it was on the banks of the Connecticut River. The appearance of the fields is pleasing to the eye, but will not bear a strict examination. We passed through one pleasant scene; descending into a valley, we approached the confluence of three branches of the Ousatonich River, which unite again into one stream. In crossing these separately a range of willows borders the causeway. The whole, united, produced a good effect. Southbury adjoining Woodbury, is much such a town; the people having acquired wealth by transporting the produce of their farms to New Haven. Newtown is situated on a hill, which commands the country for 20 miles. We perceived the town at half that distance. It is by no means a small town, and is very busy. Cloth of the first quality is made and sold very cheap, at this place. This state manufactures a great quantity of broadcloth and has arrived at great perfection. I here endeavored to exchange my saddle, but the person wishing unjustly to take advantage of my necessity, I determined to treat him as an impostor... I was very uneasy for my horse whose back, being otherwise out of order, was hurt by the smallness of the saddle. I have since met with a jockey and changed saddles. True he made me pay dear for my bargain but his prescriptions will repair the breach. The ride today has been worst than ever. Having nothing but rocks to see, the day on the whole has been tedious. This country is astonishingly well watered. Scarcely a step is passed, without having a spring in it. Scarcely a field is seen, unless watered with a refreshing brook. This is the last town in Connecticut. I have delayed giving a sketch of the character of the people, until I should see more of them. With a very few exceptions, they are rude and surly, and partake of the manners of bears. Always unwilling to oblige, when at any trouble, and the most inquisitive and officious of any people I know. This is giving them a harsh character, but is just from the knowledge I have of them. We have met with some worthy and respectful people.

The town of Danbury is very extensive. It consists, as usual, of but one street; the houses are not handsome; it has two meeting houses and a court house. It appears much like a seaport town, the street being always full of people. There are many stores and much business is transacted here. Agriculture is the most important employment, and is the source of wealth to the inhabitants. It is quite a treat to pass a few hours in such a place and reminds us of our neighboring towns at home.

PRE - CIVIL WAR CONNECTICUT

The four decades after the conclusion of the War of 1812 saw Connecticut transform itself from a predominantly agricultural society into a proto-industrial one. Steep gradients prevented most of the state's rivers from serving as convenient means of transportation, but they were admirably suited to the early phases of the industrial revolution where water was the predominant source of power. Connecticut entrepreneurs pioneered many industrial innovations in these years, and in doing so provided an alternative to emigration by the state's surplus farm population.

All but one of the passages printed below, Anne Royall's, record the observations of foreign visitors, though three of the four aliens were native English speakers. With the exception of the Pulszkys, the emerging industrial character of Connecticut's economy made little explicit impression on them. What drew their notice instead was the pastoral beauty of the state's countryside. All inadvertently recorded the effects of economic change, however, by visiting and describing the state's growing urban centers, particularly Hartford and New Haven, which provided the commercial nodes for a developing market society. Most also travelled by new forms of conveyance, steam driven vessels or the railroad, that were the harbingers of the new age.

If industrial innovation *per se* was too recent to attract these visitor's attention, several cultural developments attendant on it drew

extended commentary. Most of the visitors celebrated the state's growing cultural stature as reflected both in its luminaries of national reputation like Noah Webster, Benjamin Silliman, and Lydia Sigourney,
and in its institutions of higher education, particularly Yale. In
addition, all but the Pulszkys went out of their way to explore the
institutions spawned by the reform movements of the pre-Civil-War
period. Most of the accounts contain detailed observations of
Hartford's Retreat for the Insane and the Asylum for the Deaf and
Dumb. Those who visited Wethersfield also commented on the new
state penitentiary located there.

Two of the accounts republished below also responded to the developing enthusiasm for reform that accompanied the Second Great
Awakening. Anne Royall in her *Black Book* lamented the spread of "mis-
sionaries" throughout Connecticut, her dismissive code for the increasing number of the state's residents who identified with the revival. Edward
Abdy, on the other hand, went out of his way to criticize the way whites
treated the state's Afro-American population, perhaps on the assumption that his accusations might meet with a positive response among those
in whom the Awakening was heightening moral misgivings about the
treatment of blacks.

The Pulszkys, though the least informed of the visitors whose impressions appear in this section, nonetheless managed to capture an important dimension of the state's culture that it shared with most other
Americans at the time. In recording the warm and respectful welcome
accorded the Hungarian revolutionary Louis Kossuth throughout his
tour of the United States in the early 1850s, they bore inadvertent
witness to the continuing revolutionary identity of the nation. In cel-
ebrations honoring Kossuth, the participation of the full range of
Connecticut's people, from the factory workers at Whitneyville to
local and state dignitaries, affirmed their continuing willingness to
see contemporary revolutionary movements as related to their own
revolutionary past.

ANNE NEWPORT ROYALL

Anne Newport Royall was born in 1769 and died in 1854 at the age of 85. Her unusual longevity was more than matched by her notoriety as a writer and journalist in a time when women customarily remained in the background of public life. Her first book, the 1826 Sketches of History, Life, and Manners, in the United States, *was followed by a novel,* The Tennesseean *(1827); the Black Books of 1828 and 1829, which were continuations of her travels; accounts of other travels; and the descriptively titled* Letters from Alabama on Various Subjects: Remarks on Sundry Members of Congress...And Other High Characters At The Seat of Government *(1830).*

That Anne Royall was a most formidable woman is made clear in Virago! The Story of Anne Newport Royall, *by Alice S. Maxwell and Marion B. Dunlevy (1985). She was a confidante of none other than Andrew Jackson during his presidency, and of other well known figures. She was outspoken on the political and social issues of the day, some of her strongest attacks being leveled at "evangelists." In 1828 some of her detractors managed to bring her to trial as a "Common Scold." Though found guilty in what was widely regarded as a ludicrous trial, the 59-year-old woman was spared the prescribed punishment by ducking wheel and soon embarked on a controversial journalism career with* Paul Pry, *a weekly review in which she declared that "We shall expose all and every species of political evil, and religious fraud, without fear or affectation...We shall advocate liberty of the press, the liberty of speech, and the liberty of conscience." In her later years, famous visitors to Washington found it advantageous to pay a call on Mrs. Royall, among them Connecticut's P.T. Barnum.*

The definitive book on Anne Royall is yet to be written. Meanwhile, her own writings provide ample evidence of her powers of observation, her strong opinions, and her ability to convey both in forthright prose. The 1826 Sketches *includes an account of her journey from*

Springfield to Hartford, a lively description of the town and its inhabitants, and a similar account of New Haven. Volume II of the Black Book *contains an amusing account of a trip from Hartford (which she visited more than once) to Middletown, made by carryall via "Weathersfield" after she had missed the river boat. Her descriptions of the countryside and her frank observations of individuals and institutions offer a uniquely personal look at the social and physical landscape of the Jacksonian era.*

B. R.

1826 *Journey to Hartford, Conn.*—After amusing myself three or four days at Springfield, I sat out (in the stage again,) for Hartford, being told that it was only 18 miles, or such a matter out of the way; and that a ride down the Connecticut river, through one of the handsomest countries in the world, would richly repay me for my pains. This was enough; and with a stage full of full-blooded yankees, I set out for Hartford, keeping a south course. Nothing worth naming, occurred during the journey, which we performed in a few hours. My fellow passengers, some were ladies and some gentlemen. The conversation was desultory; banks, roads, bridges, and mercantile concerns engrossed us by turns. My attention, however, was principally engrossed by the country, in which I was not disappointed. Our course lay down the Connecticut river, which, in fertility resembles the lands on the Sciota and Miami, in the state of Ohio, rich, level, and extensive bottoms. The river appearing at intervals; the extensive meadows, orchards, and corn fields extending on both sides of the river beyond the reach of sight. The villages, the lofty white steeples of the churches, peeping up through the trees, perhaps three, four, or five miles distant, may give some idea of the scenery. We arrived at Hartford long before night, by which means we had a full prospect of the city, which mostly lies high, and presents a fine appearance as we approach it.

Excerpted from Anne Newport Royall, *Sketches of History, Life, and Manners in the United States*, printed for the author, New Haven, 1828.

"...the city...presents a fine appearance as we approach it."

—Anne Royall

HARTFORD IN 1824, ANONYMOUS, OIL ON CANVAS, N.D.

Hartford.—Hartford is a port town, in the state of Connecticut. Its form is not regular, though the streets cross each other at right angles. It lies upon the Connecticut river, and does much commercial business, the river being navigable for sloops. Every article almost is manufactured in this city; there are iron and copper foundries, gold leaf, chords, looking-glasses, stone-ware, and various other articles manufactured in Hartford. It contains a state-house, jail, circus, poor-house, work-house, retreat for the insane, American asylum for the deaf and dumb, market-house, Washington College, 3 banks, 2 fire insurance companies, 1 marine company, 1 bridge over the Connecticut river, 1 bridge over a small river in the middle of the town, 4 Congregational churches, 1 Episcopal, 1 Baptist, 1 Universalist, 1 Quaker, 4 public schools, 14 charitable and other societies, and 6,901 inhabitants, the last census. Hartford is principally built of brick. It is governed by a mayor, four aldermen, and eight common council men. The streets are paved with stone, the side-walks with flag; the streets are not lighted.

The State-House, in which the Legislature of the state hold their sessions is a very handsome plain building. The representatives' apartments are entirely void of ornament, representing one of the most striking pictures of republican simplicity. The plain seat of the speaker, the silent solemnity which reigned throughout the edifice, reminds one of the august palace of Marcus Aurelius.

Washington College is a recent establishment, not yet thoroughly in operation. It has a president, four professors, and one tutor ; several other professors are contemplated. The Rt. Rev. Thomas C. Brownell, D.D. LL. D. of Hartford, is the present president. Bishop Brownell is said to be one of the most distinguished men in New-England, in whatever light he may be considered. I attended at the college, one forenoon, to hear the students recite, and was equally surprised at their proficiency and modest deportment. The public schools of Hartford are the best regulated institutions I have seen. They are not only under able teachers, who are qualified in every branch of literature, but are under the eye of a visiting committee, who are composed of vigilant, enlightened men, whom they would find it difficult to deceive.

Poor-House.—The poor-house of Hartford is situated nearly at the extremity of the city. It is a large building, containing 48 paupers and a few refractory citizens. The keeper, Mr.—, one of the most benevolent of his species, and his wife, (one of my angels,) the most feeling, angelic, transcendently kind and charitable females, I cannot find names in our poor language, adequate to her deserts; well may the poor call her *blessed*. It is needless to consume time in describing the poor-house, after what has been said ; the condition may readily be imagined.

American Asylum.—But the glory of Hartford, and indeed that of the United States, is the American Asylum, for the education of the deaf and dumb. This asylum was incorporated in 1816; the first establishment of the sort, in the United States, and the parent of those since established, in Philadelphia and New-York. Having mentioned those asylums, now, the third time in these sketches, a brief historical outline of the art by which these unfortunate beings are instructed, may not be unwelcome to the reader. "Some years ago, a lady of Paris had two daughters that were deaf and dumb. Father Farnin, a member of the Society of Christian Doctrines, being acquainted with the lady, called at her house one day when she was out : he found no one in the house but the two deaf and dumb young ladies, and addressed several questions to them, not knowing their misfortune, to all of which they returned no answer, but studiously pursued their work, without even lifting their eyes to look at him. He attributed their silence to contempt, and withdrew in a passion, when meeting their mother at the door, he learned the cause of their silence. The circumstance filled him with emotions of pity, and from that moment he resolved to exert himself in teaching them to read and write. Death, however, surprised him before he had attained any degree of success. The first conception of a great man is generally a fruitful one. The attempt was brought to perfection under the amiable Abbe Sicard. Some few years since, the Rev. Mr. Gallaudet, a citizen of New-England, and a gentleman of distinguished merit and classical attainments, went first to England, and then to Scotland, with a view of acquiring the art of teaching the deaf and dumb. Meeting with no encouragement at either of those places, he went to France, were he was received with great kindness and respect, by Abbe Sicard. The doors of the school were thrown open to him, and being familiar with the French language, he soon returned to this country, qualified for the purpose, and bringing with him Laurent Clerc, one perfect in the science, himself being deaf and dumb. They arrived in August, 1816, and the asylum was opened in 1817. The progress of the instituition has been beyond conception:

— it is patronized by the United States, and many private gentlemen, among which I find the name of the amiable Gen. Van Rensselaer, of Albany. It is under the direction of a president, and twelve vice-presidents, for life, who are gentlemen of the first respectability in the United States. I found about 70 pupils in the asylum, some of whom were engaged in mechanical pursuits. I saw several specimens of their work, which were equal to any performed by other mechanics, such as shoes and cabinet work; but chiefly I was surprised at their literary attainments. Mr. Laurent Clerc, took me into his department, where there were about 30 pupils. He communicated to them my name, place of residence, and my pursuits. While he was doing this, their eyes were fixed on him with deep attention, and the moment he had finished, each turned to his or her slate, and in the twinkling of an eye, I saw my name, the state I was from, &c. written in a fair, legible hand; and out of the thirty there was but one letter wrong. I examined several of them, myself, by means of a slate, upon geography, grammar, history, &c. and found them perfect. The asylum is built of brick, on the finest situation in the city. It stands upon a lofty eminence which commands an extensive view of the surrounding country....

Manners and Appearance. —From what I had heard of Hartford in the western country, I expected to find a set of sour, contracted, bigoted, Pharisaical, illiberal men; the result proved quite the reverse. In their manners they are affable, open, liberal, and sociable; many of them are people of the first learning and talents. How then could they be bigoted? For politeness and easiness of address, they are inferior to no town I have visited. The ladies in these states are universally handsome as respects shape, countenance, and complexion. The ladies of Hartford, however, have a slight tinge of melancholy in their countenance; it is softened by a shade of placid tranquility. They are very delicate; but the men, particularly the laboring class, are stout and well made. They have not advanced so far yet as to countenance a theatre, though they have a circus, the next step to it. I have no doubt, but in a few years, they will extend their rational amusements as far as the stage, which may perhaps be the means of saving them from the effects of an evil which seems to threaten their morals with a total overthrow; I mean the too free use of spirituous liquors, an evil which is making fearful strides throughout the Atlantic country, and especially in port towns. Many a man, for want of amusement goes to the grog shop. Whiskey in the west, and gin in the eastern states, is to be the Caesar of America.

Amongst the number of those whose claims to particular attention are indisputable, appears our distinguished country woman Mrs. Sigourney, one of the brightest ornaments of the present age. To her we are indebted for some of the finest specimens of poetry. She is the wife of C. Sigourney, of Hartford, a gentleman of reputation, and easy fortune. This lady is richly endowed by nature, of rare personal beauty, a vigorous mind and native talent, improved far beyond her sex. But these are trifling qualities compared with her unbounded charities; diffusing comfort and pleasure to all around her; I do not know a more enviable female. Mrs. S. is above the common height of females, not too tall, she is slender with well proportioned limbs; her complexion is ruddy, with hair as black as a raven, with the finest black eye, and teeth as white as ivory. Her countenance is animated with a pleasant smile, her cheek bedecked with blushes; she shrinks from the homage paid to her virtue. She is the mother of several children, (as I have been told,) though she does not appear to be more than twenty-five years old. I found her engaged in the domestic concerns of her family; she received me with that sort of cordiality which tended no little to enhance the accounts I had received from others. I am told she is a writer of the first class in our country, but extremely averse to being known as such. Hartford seems to be a favorite soil of the feminine virtues; few cities can boast a greater number of exemplary females...

New-Haven, Conn. —Paying an occasional visit to New-Haven before this work went to press, I was led to expunge other matter in order to make room for a few remarks on that beautiful city. It stands at the head of a fine bay which sets up from Long-Island Sound; distant from New-York city 76 miles, from Boston 134, from Hartford 36, and is the semi-capital of the state of Connecticut. Its relative situation from New-York is north-east. In whatever point of view New-Haven is considered, whether for topographical beauty, the utility of its institutions, or the scenery of its environs, as a town, it is decidedly the Eden of the Union! It sits on an even plain of about three miles in circumference, which is surrounded by mountains, hills, and rugged rocks, excepting only where it faces the bay. These eminences assume an endless variety of whimsical figures, where nature seems to revel in sportive wantonness. In some places a solitary rock of stupendous dimensions presents a bold perpendicular front; others present naked bluffs of amazing height, while others meet at right angles, and run off in a thousand arbitrary directions. Some are covered with cedar and pine, others are perfectly bare; some are round craggy points. They all, however, unite in the form of an amphitheatre, by which nature evidently intended to guard her favorite spot.

These bold features of nature, contrasted with the smooth plain, covered with delicate white houses, solemn churches, lofty steeples, extensive greens, wide streets, of undeviating straitness, lined with spreading elms, and the stately buildings of Yale College, gives New-Haven an over-powering charm! Its public buildings are the Colleges, and 7 churches, viz:—2 Congragationalists, 1 Episcopalian, 1 Baptist, 1 Methodist, 2 African, 2 Banks, a court-house, (in which the Legislature sits,) a jail, an alms-house, 3 academies, 2 insurance offices, a custom-house, and 9000 inhabitants. The citizens are building a great public hotel, which is nearly completed, that for size equals, if it does not surpass, the Exchange Coffee-House in Boston. The public burying ground also deserves particular notice. The houses are mostly built of wood and painted white, with a few handsome brick buildings; the churches are also with one or two exceptions handsomely built of brick, ornamented with steeples and bells. The streets are wide, straight, and cross at right angles, each adorned with two rows of lofty elms of uncommon beauty, whose exuberant branches form a most delightful shade; almost all the houses have gardens attached to them, which are laid off in a style of inimitable taste and beauty, adorned with trees, flowers and summer houses; but its chief ornament is a great square called the green, in the centre of the city, occupying the front of the colleges. New-Haven is an incorporated town, and governed by a mayor, aldermen, and common council.

Yale College. — But New-Haven is principally distinguished for being the seat of Yale College, one of the oldest and most respectable literary institutions in the United States, and has produced some of our first men....

Yale College was founded in 1700, by a number of clergymen, and was incorporated in 1701, under ten trustees. It was first located at Saybrook in 1702; five young men received the degree of master of arts. From this period till 1718, the prosperity of the institution was greatly hindered by disputes between the trustees and the community, respecting the final establishment of the seminary. Both parties were equally disunited; but a majority of the trustees finally removed it to New-Haven in 1718. It was called Yale College out of gratitude to Elihu Yale, Esq., one of its principal benefactors. E. Yale was born in New-Haven, but left it very young for England; he afterwards went to Hindostan, where he acquired great wealth, part of which he sent to this infant college. From this period Yale College began to flourish, and in 1745 the trustees were, by a new charter, erected into a faculty of "the president and fellows of Yale College." In the mean time they received numerous donations from the colony, and private individuals also, both of this country and Europe...

Literary Men. —New-Haven is a very hot-bed of literary men. Besides several of the faculty, who have long been distinguished in the literary world. Here I met with Jedediah Morse, D.D.A.A.S. the father of American geography; also the famous Noah Webster, L.L.D. author of Webster's spelling-book, &c. &c. &c. Nothing could equal the pleasure I felt at the prospect of seeing 2 men with whose names and celebrity I had long been acquainted. Of all the Atlantic writers, these have rendered the most essential benefit to the western country: and the first person I called

on in New-Haven, was the Rev. J. Morse, whom I had long since thought
was numbered with the dead. I found him, however, alive and well; quite
a lively and genteel man, not only polite, but friendly, sociable, and con-
descending; nor does he look so old as one would expect. Mr. M. in his
person is rather over than under six feet in height, remarkably slender
and straight; he appears a little turned of seventy; his visage is thin, long,
and features rather delicate, with a fine, full dark eye; his hair is plen-
tiful, parted from the crown to the forehead, and drops off on each side;
it is gray but not perfectly white; his head is remarkably small, rather
more oval than common. He is quite an active man for his years, and
still pursues writing geographies; but our country increases so fast, that
the old gentleman hardly gets one geography out before it is out of date,
and he has to commence anew. He speaks very slow and soft, without
the least ostentation of learning. I called upon him often in his study,
and found him always pleasant and communicative; he lives in plain style;
his first wife is living, and quite as agreeable in her manners as her husband. He told me he had three sons living in New-York, and one on his
travels in Europe. He dresses in a plain gown, and looks very venerable. After Mr. M., the next man I called on was the celebrated Mr. W.
I knocked at the door with more than common enthusiasm; for though
we back-woods folks are not learned ourselves, we have a warm liking
for learned people. In a few minutes, a low chubby man, with a haughty
air, stepped into the room; his face was round and red, and by no means
literary looking. He was dressed in black broadcloth, in dandy style; in
short, he comes nearer the description of a London cockney, than any
character I can think of; he eyed me with ineffable scorn, and scarcely
deigned to speak at all. I am sorry for his sake I ever saw the man, as it
gave me infinite pain to rescind an opinion I had long entertained of
him. He appears to be about sixty years of age.

The next person I waited upon was President Day, who gave me a reception worthy the principal of Yale College. This celebrated man is of middle age, tall, and well made; his complexion inclining to dark, his face is

oval, with a keen hazel eye, his countenance grave and dignified, and plainly marked with the lines of deep thinking; his features are regularly proportioned, manly and striking, with a high smooth forehead; his manners are those of a perfect gentleman. With respect to President Day's natural and acquired abilities, it is superfluous to say any thing, as he is universally known, to be a man of general science, and one of the first mathematicians of the present age. Professor Silliman is in appearance very like President Day, about the same age and size; his complexion fairer, with the same hazel eye, but a shade darker, sparkling with genius; his countenance more luminous and striking, and his manners more captivating. As a writer, chemist, and mineralogist, Professor Silliman ranks among the first men of this or of any other country. He visited Europe when a young man, with a view of prosecuting his studies, particularly of chemistry, where he travelled three years; during which he wrote a journal of his travels, a rare and invaluable work, which does honor to the American character. His remarks in this work are concise, but pointed, and display the most striking evidence of talent, industry, and research, to be found; nothing dry nor volatile, not a line in the whole work, which is considerable, but conveys both pleasure and instruction. He delivers lectures on chemistry in Yale College, during the winter months, which, for elocution, science and sentiment, are said to afford a perfect intellectual feast.

৵ BASIL HALL ৵

W*hen Captain Basil Hall visited the United States in 1827 and 1828 the young British naval officer had already built a modest reputation as a travel writer with the publication of a two(volume description of the three years (1820-22) that he spent in Chili, Peru, and Mexico. His fourteen month sojourn in North America, though shorter in duration than his earlier stay in South America, was even more ambitious because he was accompanied by his wife Margaret, whose account* *of the trip, entitled* The Aristocratic Journey, *was ultimately published in 1931, and the couple's infant daughter. Armed with letters of introduction to more than one hundred prominent Americans, the Halls did not let family responsibilities limit their mobility. After exploring New England and New York State they followed an arduous circular route through Philadelphia, Baltimore, Washington, Norfolk, Charleston, and Savannah to New Orleans before heading up the Mississippi River to the Ohio valley and back to the East coast.*

The Halls' exploration of Connecticut came early in their trip, in October 1827, and was brief, lasting less than one week. They came from Providence by public stage to Hartford "over a rugged, hilly, disagreeable road as ever was seen," making stops in Brooklyn, Windham, and Coventry, a trip of 72 miles that they completed in fifteen hours. After spending a busy day in Hartford, the Hall family set off for New Haven via Middletown. They spent two more days in New Haven in the company of intellectuals such as Benjamin Silliman and Noah Webster before booking a steamer to New York City. Basil Hall was often patronizing toward American culture. He was horrified, for example, at the crudity of the table manners of the students at Captain Partridge's Military Seminary in Middletown. However, like most early nineteenth-century visitors, he admired Connecticut's public institutions. The single day he spent in the Hartford region was devoted to tours of the new State Prison at Wethersfield, the Asylum for the Deaf and Dumb, and the Retreat for the Insane, both in Hartford. He judged "all of first rate excellence in their respective lines."

H.J.

1827 The nominal hour of starting, was five in the morning; but as every thing in America comes sooner than one expects, a great tall man walked into the room at ten minutes before four

Excerpted from Basil Hall, *Travel in North America in the years 1827 and 1828*, (2 vols.). Philadelphia, Carey, Lea, and Carey, 1829 o'clock, to say it wanted half an hour of five; and presently we heard the rumbling of the stage coming to the door, upwards of thirty minutes before the time specified.

Fortunately, there were only five passengers, so that we had plenty of room; and as the morning was fine, we might have enjoyed the journey much, had we not been compelled to start so miserably early. At the village of Windham, we dined in a cheerful sunny parlour, on a neatly dressed repast, excellent in every way, and with very pleasant, chatty company. The whole dinner party were absorbed in vehement discussions respecting the endless presidential question, which in country as well as in town, appeared to occupy all men's minds, morning, noon, and night. I joined as well as I could in these conversations, though sorely perplexed in trying to follow the rambling nature of these New Englanders' talk; for they wandered from the topic to the right and to the left in such a way, that I often quite lost sight of the original point. They were extremely bitter against General Jackson, one of the candidates; but what I then thought odd enough, they were not much more favourably disposed, individually, to Mr. Adams, his opponent.

We made out our seventy-two miles in fourteen hours and a half, or nearly five miles an hour, over a rugged, hilly, disagreeable road as ever was seen. When going up the steep parts, the pace was very slow; but to compensate for this, we generally galloped down; and frequently, also, when the ascent was short, made a noisy canter of it, right up. At every four or five miles, we stopped to water the horses, and to give out and take in the mail-bags, which were never ready at the post-office. Then we had the most troublesome of all jobs to go through, that of changing coaches, no less than four times; all these things, together with frequent stops to have a gossip and a glass of brandy made the day seem endless.

In the course of the 25th of October, spent at and near Hartford in Connecticut, we visited three very important public establishments, all of first rate excellence in their respective lines. The State Prison, the Asylum for the Deaf and Dumb, and the Institution for the Insane. The prison, or penitentiary, is upon the Auburn plan already described, where the separation of the convicts at night is complete—hard labour and silence are rigorously enforced throughout the day—solitary meals in the cells—and where all social intercourse is effectually interdicted [except] with the resident clergyman, on Sundays....

The Asylum for the Deaf and Dumb at Hartford has the merit of being the earliest institution of the kind established in America. It is under admirable management; but there is nothing respecting it so peculiar as to call for particular notice.

In one of the rooms we saw a very interesting person, a young woman born deaf, blind, and dumb. It appeared that some of the other girls had been trying to bring her to the room in which we were standing, which attempts had discomposed her wonted serenity a little, for the expression of her countenance was at first by no means agreeable. But in a few minutes Mr. Gallaudett, the benevolent and able manager of the establishment, by patting her gently on the cheek, pressing her hands between his, and using other little blandishments which he knew were pleasing to her, gradually brought a smile to her lips, and then, certainly, the expression of her countenance was most engaging. She took our hands, felt our clothes minutely, took my watch in her hand, examined the chain and seals, and seemed desirous of showing that she knew how to wind it up. A needle and thread was brought, which she threaded by the assistance of her tongue, after four or five ineffectual attempts.

While looking at a creature differing from ourselves in so many respects, we are tempted to ask, what can a mind so circumstanced be thinking of? What images—what combinations of ideas can it be contemplating?... It is true, there was no idiocy in this case, on the contrary evidently the workings of regulated intellect; but how regulated? or how employed? were questions utterly beyond the reach of human research....

Our last visit was to the Connecticut Retreat for the Insane. The title given to it will recall the celebrated establishment for the same benevolent purpose at York. At Hartford, however, the moral treatment, and the system of gentleness, are carried even still farther, as I understand, than in England.

Many persons approach this subject with disgust—some with apprehension—and all, or nearly all, when they first come into actual contact with it, with feelings of great uneasiness. A little resolute practice, however, soon banishes these unworthy considerations, or it reduces them within all the control that is necessary for any useful investigation of the subject. At least so I found it in America, for though I could never bring myself to examine such places at home, the difficulty vanished when the trial was actually made as a matter of duty. But I speak upon this, and upon many other points in these American inquiries, with much and sincere distrust of my own conclusions. The mere wish to see and to represent faithfully is not enough. It is not very easy, in the first place, to get at every thing we ought to examine in such places, in order to form a right judgment upon the question in hand. We have often not time, and still more frequently have not sufficient preparatory knowledge, to make the proper inquiries. And even when in presence of the things we have been seeking for, how difficult is it to look at them aright! It will not unfrequently happen, too, that a casual misconception of a fact, sends us away with more error than knowledge; and I have sometimes seen people of a good sense, visit the same institution on the same day, and even in the same company, and yet leave it impressed with very opposite opinions.

Dr. Todd, the eminent and kind physician in charge of the retreat, gladly communicated his plans, and showed us over every part of this noble establishment,—a model, I venture to say, from which any country might take instruction. The institutions at Hartford, which, indeed, are not to be excelled any where, not only do high honour to this part of the union, but are every way creditable to the nation generally.

"...this noble establishment—a model...from which any country might take instruction." (page 97)

—Basil Hall

Dr. Todd's method is to treat every insane patient as if he were a reasonable being. This would be useless, of course, as applied to idiocy, or that class which bears the terrible name of Mania Ferox; but even with them he observes the same principle as much as possible. When a patient is brought to the retreat, the physician converses with him freely; and, without attempting to deceive, states all that is known of his case, explains that he is brought there for the purpose of being cured of a disease which happens to affect his mind, as it might have done his body; that he will have every possible freedom consistent with his own safety, and the comfort of his friends; but that he must conform exactly to the regulations established for the good order of the house.

The same cordial, unreserved system is pursued from first to last; and even if there be no cure in the end, still it must diminish greatly the misery of the patients. Nor need I observe how much a knowledge of this fact is calculated to alleviate the affliction of friends, who, after all, may often be the parties most in need of commiseration.

In practical illustration of this system, Dr. Todd carried us to a neatly finished parlour, where we found eight or ten females seated at their work. Instead of showing them off like monsters, he introduced us to each of them, and encouraged conversation as if all the company had been in perfect health....

On the 26th of October we proceeded to New Haven, which is also on the Connecticut, and is considered, alternately with Hartford, the capital of the state; for the legislature meet first at one place, and the next year at the other. This clumsy arrangement requires the annual transfer backwards and forwards of all the records and other papers, to which reference has to be made during the session. It reminds one of those old times, when parliament met one session at Oxford, the next in London.

We visited on our way an establishment recently set a-going by a very spirited private individual, in rivalry of the celebrated Military Seminary at West Point, which, as I have mentioned before, is supported at the public expense. The founder and manager was absent, but the professor of mathematics received us most kindly; and under his guidance we inspected the different parts of his establishment, which, though not yet equal to its model is highly creditable to the skill and industry of the projector. While we were talking in the court-yard, dinner was announced; and the professor begging us to walk with him, we entered the great hall together. The principal body of the young men, assembled on the exercising ground, were marched to dinner, to the sound of drum and fife, in very good order. About a dozen of the students, however, were first admitted as carvers, and I stood in perfect astonishment at the scene which ensued.

In all countries, old as well as new, gentlemen, to their shame be it said, carve abominably ill; but I had no expectations of seeing any thing so primitive as what now took place. The meat was literally hacked and torn to pieces. In a few minutes afterwards, at a given signal, the other students entered, and there commenced such an exhibition of feeding— or devouring, I may call it, as would have excited the admiration of a cormorant. Some of the youths were spooning great lumps of meat down their throats with their knives, while others helped themselves, two or three at a time, with their own knives and forks, from the same dish! I really never saw any thing so disagreeable.

I relate these circumstances, not certainly for any purpose of ridicule, nor as a matter of mere curiosity, but in the hope that the disinterested remarks of a stranger may contribute in some degree to remedy so grievous a defect in good breeding, as that just described. It will be observed, that I have, up to this moment, studiously avoided making allusions in my narrative to any of those points in domestic manners which, in consequence of the difference between American and English usages, appear repugnant to our tastes. But I hope that in speaking of this public establishment, I shall have given no offence, by taking notice of an evil which might so easily be remedied. In what respect, it may be asked, would the studies, and other pursuits of young men at these military and literary seminaries, be injured be requiring of them to cut their meat decently, and eat it leisurely? Or from making it imperative upon them to deport themselves at table, according to those rules and customs established, as matters of course, amongst gentlemen in every other civilized part of the world?

Next day, we did a good deal of duty in the way of sightseeing at New Haven. Our guide was Professor Silliman—a gentleman well known to the scientific world as editor of a valuable philosophical journal, which bears his name.

Yale College, of course, was the chief object of attraction; and it was extremely agreeable to see so many good old usages and orthodox notions kept up as rigorously, all things considered, as possible. How long the able and zealous professors of this celebrated establishment will be able to stem effectually that deluge of innovation and would-be improvements in doctrine, discipline, and pursuits, which is sweeping over the rest of the country, and obliterating so many of the land-marks of experience, I cannot pretend to say. Meanwhile, every thing that came under my notice, seemed judiciously regulated. The courses of study were apparently well managed, and the period required was rather longer than we had heard spoken of in other places. But there is here, I suspect, as in

every other institution in America, almost insuperable difficulty in pre-
vailing upon the persons, essentially most interested, to remain long
enough in training before they start in the vehement race of busy life.

After an early dinner, we drove out of the town to the grave-yard, one
of the prettiest burying places I ever saw. It occupies an area of twenty
acres, laid out in avenues, and divided by rows of trees into lots for the
different inhabitants. These connecting lanes or roads are not gravelled,
but laid down in grass, as well as the intermediate spaces, which are spot-
ted over with handsome monuments of all sizes and forms, giving a lively
instead of a gloomy air, to the whole scene.

There is certainly some improvement in this, compared with the practice of huddling together so many graves in the confined space round
the places of worship in a populous city. The idea of death and its earthly
consequences is said, and probably with truth, to aid the purposes of
religion. But it surely does not follow, that these purposes are less use-
fully served in such a cheerful place as I have been describing, than by
the associations connected with a soppy churchyard, where the mourn-
ers sink ankle-deep in a rank and offensive mould, mixed up with broken bones and fragments of coffins; or that the cause of virtue is
advanced by the recollection of coughs, colds, and rheumatisms out of
number, caught whilst half a dozen old fellows, with long-tailed,
threadbare black coats, are filling up a grave, for which they themselves
might seem the readiest tenants.

It was a biting cold day—but the sun shone out pleasantly on sea and
land, and brightened up the last dying tints of the autumn. After an amusing scramble, we gained the brow of a basaltic ridge facing the south,
exactly resembling in its geological character, in height, and picturesque appearance, the well-known cliff called Salisbury Crags near
Edinburgh. The only difference which I could discover was in this ridge
being clad with a forest of young oak-trees, amongst which the Cactus,
or prickly pear, was growing in great luxuriance.

Our next visit was to a place of considerable interest, and much cel-

The Connecticut Historical Society, Hartford.

"...their place of security was a dark cavern formed by the overhanging rocks..."
—Basil Hall

JUDGE'S CAVE, NEW HAVEN, ANONYMOUS. PHOTOGRAPH, N.D.

ebrated in the early histories of America. It seems that three of those
bold men who sat in judgment upon their king, were driven to New England
in 1660, after the Restoration, and, during the anxious period which succeeded, when their blood was eagerly sought for, they were often compelled to fly to the interior—then a complete wilderness. It is generally believed that their place of security was a dark cavern, formed by
the overhanging rocks, a mile or two to the eastward of the cliffs just
mentioned. The names of these regicides were Goffe, Whalley, and Dixwell,
and their retreat is still called the Judge's Cave.

In the evening I had the pleasure of being introduced to Mr. Noah
Webster, of New Haven, a gentleman who has been occupied during
the last forty years of his life in preparing a dictionary of the English
language, which, I find, has since been published. He includes in it all
the technical expressions connected with the arts and sciences. Thus
giving, he hopes, as complete a picture as possible of the English language, as it stands at this moment, on both sides of the Atlantic.

We had a pleasant discussion on the use of what are called
Americanisms, during which he gave me some new views on this subject. He contended that his countrymen had not only a right to adopt
new words, but were obliged to modify the language to suit the novelty of the circumstances, geographical and political, in which they were
placed. He fully agreed with me, however, in saying, that where there
was an equally expressive English word, cut and dry, it ought to be used
in preference to a new one. "Nevertheless," said he, "it is quite impossible to stop the progress of language—it is like the course of the Mississippi,
the motion of which, at times, is scarcely perceptible; yet even then it
possesses a momentum quite irresistible. It is the same with the language we are speaking of. Words and expressions will be forced into use,
in spite of all the exertions of all the writers in the world."...

On the 29th October, we proceeded in a steam-boat from New
Haven, down what is called Long Island Sound, and through the well-
known narrow pass which bears the ominous name of Hell's Gates.

103

❧ EDWARD STRUTT ABDY ❧

A Fellow of Jesus College, Cambridge, Edward Strutt Abdy came to America at the age of 42 sent by the British government to inspect and report on prisons and asylums. When that work was finished and his partners returned to England, he stayed on to investigate more fully and report on the rampant racism that made a strong impression on him.

Among the public figures writing and preaching against slavery in the early nineteenth century was William Ellery Channing, minister of Boston's Federal Street Congregational Church. His progressive views on various subjects are said to have influenced Emerson, Holmes, and Bryant, and his lucid writings on slavery helped prepare for emancipation. In a 1966 article in American Quarterly, *Thomas F. Harwood suggests that Channing's convictions on the immorality of slavery crystallized after his meeting with Abdy, who traveled in the United States in 1833 and 1834. Although Channing never directly allied himself with the abolitionists, the penetrating questions Abdy put to him in their conversation are thought to have motivated Channing to oppose slaveholding much more forcefully in his preaching and writing.*

Though reporting on other matters as well, Abdy's three-volume Journal of a Residence and Tour in the United States of North America *is devoted principally to the "peculiar instituition," a fact suggested by the quotation from Daniel Webster on the title page of each of its three volumes:*

> *As far as experience may shew errors in our establishments, we are bound to correct them; and, if any practices exist contrary to the principles of justice and humanity, within the reach of our laws or our influence, we are inexcusable if we do not exert ourselves to restrain and abolish them.*

For all of Abdy's thoroughgoing condemnation of the evils of racial prejudice and slavery, he writes with affection of the countryside he sees

*and the people he interviews. He found much to admire in our prisons
and asylums. He wrote little else, and died in 1846. A posthumous second edition of the* Journal *in 1849 joined the ever growing stream of
anti-slavery literature that by 1852 would include Harriet Beecher Stowe's*
Uncle Tom's Cabin.

B. R.

1833

July 10th. I left New York for Hartford in Connecticut
with Mr. Crawford (the Commissioner for inspecting the prisons) and
his coadjutor Mr. Newman. We went by the steam-boat to New Haven,
(eighty-four miles,) and the rest of the way (about forty) by stage. The
whole fare (by sea and land) was three dollars each. It was eight
o'clock P.M. when we arrived at the end of our journey, having started
at seven in the morning,—New Haven—a very beautiful town, with many
well-built houses and neat gardens. I had afterwards an opportunity of
revisiting it. We passed through a delightful country, more remarkable,
however, for picturesque scenery than fertility of soil; some of the towns
on the road, particularly Middletown on the Connecticut river, are well
chosen for salubrity of air, cheerfulness of situation, and beauty of prospect.

At the hotel where we put up, the first on entering Hartford, we found
everything extremely good. The rooms were clean and well furnished,
and the people of the house particularly civil. The next day we proceeded
to the prison at Weathersfield, four miles from Hartford. The plan, on
which it is built, and the system, upon which it is conducted, are something similar to those at Singsing; except that the prison is much less
in extent, and the discipline milder. No flogging is used for breach of
rules. A diet of bread and water, with solitary confinement in a dark cell,
is found to bring the most refractory to reason in a very short time. It
should be observed, that the time thus spent by the convict is added
to the term of his imprisonment. He has therefore a direct interest in
shortening its duration. Add to this consideration, that every prisoner

Excerpted from Edward Strutt Abdy, *Journal of a Residence and Tour in the United States of North
America...*, London, John Murray, 1835.

is charged, on his entrance, with the expenses of arrest, prosecution, &c.: amounting, on an average, to 100 dollars. This debt he is made to work out, should he be guilty of any misconduct. These little auxiliaries to the ordinary motives for good conduct lessen the chances of disobedience. The number of cells for male prisoners is 236, and that for females 32. Of the former there were 187; and of the latter 14. The "cat", though allowed by law, is never employed by the warden; a man who unites great firmness of character with mildness of deposition; and who has now an additional stimulus for vigilance and attention to his official duties in the injustice with which he has been treated, having been displaced by the basest intrigue—an event that too often befalls this class of functionaries in many of the States. At the period of our visit, he had just been reinstated, in the most honorable manner, after an absence of nine months, during which the laxity of discipline, that ensued, cost his life to one of the keepers, who was murdered in attempting to prevent the escape of four convicts: two of the murderers were then under sentence of death for the crime. The proceeds from the labor of the convicts more than cover the expenditure of the establishment. There are no outer walls to the prison: to prevent escape, two guards with rifles parade the rampart or projection, that overlooks the yard, and commands every part of the building. Two or three, at the first establishment, attempted to make their escape, but were retaken. It seems hardly justifiable to subject a man to the penalty of death for obeying a natural impulse, and to inflict the same punishment for an offence, without regard to the character of the offender, or the consequences of his guilt. The proportion of free blacks among the convicts is about twenty or twenty-five per cent., while they form but three per cent. upon the whole population of the State. This difference may be accounted for by the greater degree of temptation to which they are exposed, and the little encouragement they receive to good conduct. To be excluded, directly or virtually, from many employments, (for the whites will not work with them,) and to be despised in all, affords but sorry inducements to honesty and self-correction. What attachment can they have to virtue, when it affords them no protection, and meets with no reward? How can those, who are disposed to crime, retain their honesty, when they see the honest treated like criminals? How singular is the policy of this country! On one hand it prepares men for the penitentiary, while on the other it is laboring at the diminution of crime, and the reformation of offenders. But what shall we say of its justice, which thus forces its subjects into by-paths, and then punishes them for the deviation? Crime, of course, increases, as the motives to good conduct are removed, and the means of an honest livelihood refused. The same principle may be seen in the manufacturing districts of France and England; where the criminal calender is found to swell with the pressure of commercial distress, and diminish with its removal. It is a trick of very long standing to refuse straw to the brickmakers, and then exclaim against them—ye are idle! ye are idle! Among the blacks was a native of St. Domingo, and formerly one of Napoleon's Mamelukes. He had been condemned, about three months before, for adultery with a woman, who, he declared, had deceived him by concealing her marriage. Adultery is considered in the State of Connecticut a civil offence, and is punished by imprisonment.

Of the different trades here pursued, some of the contractors (shoe-makers, for instance) require a certain quantity of work from those under them. If it is completed within the time, the rest of the week belongs to them; when they are paid for extra labor, and the money is delivered to the warden, who makes it over to them when the term of their confinement has expired; or, if they wish it, transmits it to their families. A colored man had just informed the chaplain, from whom I had this account, that he had finished his week on the preceding Tuesday. One observation the chaplain made struck me as singular; he said, that the generality of convicts were, in point of intellect, below mediocrity....

Here my fellow-travellers left me; and we agreed to meet again at Boston. In the afternoon, I called on Mr. Wadsworth, a relative of the gentleman from whom I had received so much attention at New York.

He received me with that urbanity and kindness, which are habitual to men of gentlemanly feelings and an amiable disposition. He belonged to an old and wealthy family, that had long been settled in the country. Our conversation turned upon the social economy, that prevailed in the land of his birth. His remarks upon the rank, which servants hold there, and the treatment best adapted to their condition and expectations, were highly interesting and just. For nearly forty years, that he had kept house, he had found, he told me, but one domestic who had proved dishonest or unfaithful. He had met with no disrespect from them, for he had never shewn any towards them. They were attached to him, because he was indulgent to them; and obedient, because their services were neither exacted with rigor, nor received with indifference. The next morning, he took me in his gig to the Retreat for the Insane, of which he was a director. On our way, we turned a little out of our road, to visit the famous old oak, where the charter, on which the Colony was founded, was concealed in 1686 by a lineal ancestor of Mr. Wadsworth. The hole, into which it was put, is now closed over. The tree, however, is in full vigor, and likely to survive many years. That arbitrary power, the baneful effects of which are presented to the mind by the sight of this tree, cost the monarch his crown, and one of his successors its "brightest jewel." What will it cost this great confederation, when it is wrested from the hands of the slave-owner? The house, in the grounds attached to which the charter-oak stands, belongs to a man who made a considerable fortune as a shopkeeper in Charleston. Not having much taste or inclination for laying out grounds or improving his fields, he has sadly neglected the place. It commands a fine view of the country beyond the river, and might, with little trouble or expense, be made a very agreeable spot. A man of color, who happened to be in the garden, shewed me the grounds, while my "guide, philosopher, and friend" remained in the gig. Upon my asking the man, how his brethren were treated in the town, he replied that they were insulted and annoyed in a very shameful manner. Frequent broils and fights were the consequence; and the bitter feeling of animosity, that existed against them, had much increased since the Colonization Society had become more active.

After this, we proceeded to the Retreat, on arriving at which we found that the superintendant, Dr. Todd, was out. An officer of the institution, however, conducted us over the building, and explained its details.... No kind of deception, and, if possible, no restraint, is exercised upon the patients, who are allowed every indulgence and gratification that are not incompatible with the object for which they are sent hither. They are informed, on their first arrival, that they are laboring under some disease, which has affected their minds, and requires peculiar treatment.... With the aid of soothing language, occupation suited to their inclinations, proper exercise, and appropriate medicines, an alleviation, if not a cure, of the malady is effected.... No one is confined, however violent or intractable, in irons or in solitude. No breach of promise, no attempt to mislead, is ever permitted. The little glimmering of reason, that remains even in the worst cases, is skilfully employed by the keepers and assistants to lead the sufferer into feelings and habits, that at last conduct him to a clearer sky, if not into open day. "Let gentleness my strong enforcement be", seems to be the guiding rule to all who are to co-operate in carrying this principle into practice....

Riding on horseback for both sexes is found very serviceable: gardening, or any other occupation that may interest or amuse, is employed with good effect; and, as the house is open to visitors at all times, and the same courtesies are observed towards the inmates as are practised in common life, a constant succession of objects presents itself, to give gentle exercise to the tastes and affections, and dispel the morbid illusions of the imagination. To gain his confidence, and imperceptibly lead him to the exercise of its disused energies and faculties—"waking thoughts that long had slept"—is all that the physician studies in the management of his patient, who seems to give to candor and conciliatory mildness those affections and regards, which harshness and distrust had driven from their natural channels. The patients attend their respective places of worship, when not incapacitated by the nature of the malady, under which they labor. This is considered an indulgence; and, as it may be withdrawn on disobedience or infringement of the conditions on which it is granted, an additional motive for self-restraint is obtained, beyond what may be expected from attendance on public worship in the house. The wish to be admitted, in common with those who are in good health, and the apprehension of being thought undeserving of that privilege, are powerful inducements with persons, who find their comforts to depend upon their conformity with the will of their attendants. Whenever it is necessary to put a strait-waistcoat upon a patient, it is done, if possible, with his consent. He is told that the excitement under which he suffers may be considered as the work of an enemy, and not the result of any voluntary action of his own mind, for which he would, if in sound health, be responsible; and that self-defence requires and excuses a precaution that might otherwise appear degrading....

Not many months after my visit to this interesting spot, the intelligence, which had shed its healing influence upon it, had returned to its kindred spirits. Dr. Todd had terminated his earthly career. His loss may be viewed in the light of a national calamity.... One little anecdote I was told of him will give a good idea of the quickness and sagacity, with which he converted any minute incident or feeling to his own purposes. One of the female patients put her head out of the window one night, and commenced uttering the most horrid screams and cries imaginable. Throwing up the sash suddenly, and putting his head out of the window,—he called out in a loud voice:— "Is that you, Mary, making such a noise?—I could not have believed it! Here have I been working all day for you, and the rest of the house; and to-morrow I have a great deal to do. It is very hard that you thus disturb my rest." "Doctor!" she replied, "I beg your pardon most sincerely; if I had thought I was disturbing you, I would not have made any noise for the world." She immediately retired to her bed; and all was quiet again....

The next day Mr. Wadsworth drove me over in his gig to Monte Video—
a very beautiful place belonging to him, about ten miles from Hartford.
We passed through a fine country, studded with farm-houses, and
resembling England in its fields and enclosures. The grounds surrounding
the villa, were, before they came into the possession of the present owner,
a wild and impassable forest; the approach to which was so difficult and
dangerous as to require a whole day to visit the mountain from the city.
It took twenty men two years to clear away the wood and make the road.
Three thousand loads of stone were precipitated into the valley
beneath, before the work was completed. The proprietor has been well
repaid for the trouble and expenditure of the undertaking. A nobler view,
than is here presented on each side of the mountain, is rarely to be met
with. On the west is seen a considerable part of the State of Connecticut,
with the Farmington dividing the valley with its woody banks; on the
opposite side, Massachusetts beyond the Connecticut river; and
towards the north-east the view stretches into the States of New York
and New Hampshire: the one presenting the mountain Taghkonic, the
western branch of the green mountains; and the other Monadnock, distant about ninety miles. Beneath your feet, whichever way you turn,
is a foreground of the finest forest scenery. The house is merely a summer residence for two or three months during the sultry season. It was
at first but a small cabin; and has become, by successive additions, what
it is at present—a small but convenient cottage—suited to the modest
wants of the proprietor, and large enough for the claims and pleasures
of hospitality. Nature had done every thing for this beautiful eminence;
and asked but the hand of art to remove the obstructions to her temple: and well has the task been performed. There is no misplaced ornament, and no attempt to surprise the spectator by unexpected contrast,
or artificial embellishment. The only deviation from the rigid observance of simplicity is in the erection of a wooden tower on one of the
summits, into which the ridge of rock seems to have been abruptly broken by some great convulsion of nature—a shock that has left between

the corresponding heights one of the most charming features of the scene—a lake of pure and transparent water. The opposite summit consists of bare and crumbling rock; and, being the first visited, presents at once a view of the lake, the house and grounds, and the distant prospect, which is terminated by the horizon.

The top of the tower, which is hexagonal, is 960 feet above the Connecticut. The house is 640 feet above the Farmington. The place reminded me strongly of the grounds belonging to Colonel Maclean (Coll) near Tobermory in the isle of Mull. There were equal difficulties to contend with in both cases. As the latter, however, resides on the spot, he has taken more pains to improve the garden and plantations. Scott's description of Loch Katrine in his Lady of the Lake, might be applied to much of the scenery at this place—my amiable cicerone, who had an excellent memory and great literary taste, repeated the whole to me, as we stood on one of the points that overlook the lake; and marked with his finger, as he proceeded, the singular coincidences and resemblances, that were to be found in the imagination of the poet and the various objects that lay before us and around us. While standing on the top of the tower, and surveying the noble prospect below, I could not but reflect how many happy human beings its circumference embraced; and how few are the eminences in Europe, distracted by the fears and hopes of revolutionary changes, whence one could look down on an equal quantity of comfort and contentment.

In the evening, after drinking tea with the family, and conversing with several agreeable persons who called, as is at Hartford and elsewhere the "custom always in the afternoon," I went into a confectioner's shop in the town to get some ice, and was shewn into an inner room, where I found the master of the house, reclining at his ease upon a sofa. He made no movement to rise; nor appeared to take any notice of my entrance. The competition, it was plain, was more among the buyers than the sellers; and in fact, as the weather was oppressively hot, I stood more in need of his ice, than he of my money. While the young woman who assisted,

"...a view of the lake, the house and grounds, and the distant prospect..."
—Edward Abdy

MONTE VIDEO: APPROACH TO THE HOUSE, BY S.S. JOCELYN AFTER D. WADSWORTH.
ENGRAVING, N.D.

was getting what I had asked for, I entered into conversation with him; and found him very obliging and civil. Perceiving I was an Englishman, he was anxious to hear how matters were going on in the old country, and his questions were readily answered. A neighbour coming in, our talk continued for some time; and when I took my leave he begged I would call again, and have some more chat with him. Nothing was further from his thoughts than to mortify me by any appearance of slight or inattention:—nor was I disappointed at not meeting with that assiduity and obsequiousness, which self-interest would have prompted a London tradesman to display before a customer, and which would have been as little connected with real respect, as my Hartford friend's nonchalance with rudeness or ill-manners.

❧ FRANCIS AND THERESA PULSKY ❧

*F*rancis and Theresa Pulsky accompanied Lajos (Louis) Kossuth on
his tour through the United States in 1851-1852. His visit was in
response to a joint congressional resolution, said by Francis Pulsky to
have been offered just once before, to Lafayette. The Hungarian patriot
who led and inspired Hungary's struggle for independence from Austria
had only a brief period of power in 1848 and 1849, but Kossuth
aroused widspread support for his revolutionary causes. From the moment
of his landing in New York in December 1851, he received great ovations,
and in touring with him, the Pulskys were afforded "more facility of becoming familiar with the policy and society of the New World, than is granted
to most travelers." In his foreword, Pulsky declared that foreigners to
Great Britain and America could be more impartial in viewing the United
States than "the son of the mother-country, attached to her manners and
customs." Their viewpoints, he wrote, would not have the fault of many
travel books that dwell on insignificant discrepancies between America
and Great Britain. He observed that English publications were "accustomed to underrate the development of Americans and the character of
her citizens, except in regard to commerce." Mr. Pulsky also credited co-
authorship with his wife, who kept a regular diary of their travels, "the
greater part of which has been incorporated in this publication."

On April 1852 the Kossuth party took the train to Connecticut, a state
"founded on religious principles, not on love of lucre." Their only major
stop was in New Haven, where the city officials greeted Kossuth on the
steps of the old State House on the Green. From there they went to the
Whitney gun factory in Whitneyville, Hamden, to receive from the workmen a gift of twenty-five rifles for the Hungarian cause. After dining
with the Mayor, they boarded the train bound for Springfield, stopping
briefly at Hartford and other stations where Kossuth addressed the "enthusiastic crowds gathered round the cars."

J. S.

1852   We soon entered Connecticut, the state which, like
Massachusetts, was founded on religious principles, not on love of lucre,
by men who began their settlements, not with a trading post defended
by a fort, but with the church and the school-house; by men accustomed
not to yield passively to authority, but to govern themselves in their
own way by the will of the majority, and who declared that the word
of God should be the sole rule for regulating the affairs of the commonwealth. They did not reason much about the abstract principles
of freedom, they enacted several restrictive laws regulating the manners and customs of the people, and interfering with their dress and
amusements, but they never did it against the will of the majority, and
this spirit seems not yet extinct; the agitation for the Maine liquor law,
which prohibits the sale of spirits of every description, bears evidence
in this respect. I had heard that the Yankees are sacrificing every feeling to gain, and bending every faculty to acquisition; but I found myself
agreeably surprised by the charming appearance of New Haven,
with its broad places, and the magnificent double alley of elms,
which, forming a vault with their branches, resemble a gigantic
cathedral with two side aisles round their nave. The court-house, an
elegant building, facing an extensive meadow, was the place where
the city authorities addressed Kossuth under the colonnade, to which
a broad staircase leads from the green field below, crowded by a respect-
fully listening multitude. From the opposite window of the hotel where
I was seated, the view was gay and brilliant. After the reception, we
visited the stately Yale College, founded in the beginning of the last
century, by Elihu Yale, a native of New Haven, who had acquired a
large estate in the East Indies, married an Indian lady of fortune, and
had become Governor of the East India Company in London. Another
son of this State, Colonel Trumball, the friend of Washington,
bequeathed his own paintings to the college. Though they are not of
great artistical value, they have the highest importance for every American,
as they contain about 250 portraits of persons distinguished in the American

Excerpted from Francis and Theresa Pulsky, *White, Red, and Black: Sketches of American Society in the
United States During the Visit of their Guests...*, (2 vols.), New York, Redfield, 1853.

Revolution, painted by him from life. The larger compositions are devoted to the principal events of that memorable period, and a series of them has been executed by the Colonel in a larger size for the rotunda of the capitol at Washington. Though the correctness of his design is not unexceptionable, and his coloring less glowing than his patriotism, yet this gallery is a fine historical monument.

We proceeded thence to Whitneyville—the large musket manufactory of Mr. Whitney—through a picturesque valley, watered by a fine stream, and bordered on one side by rocky heights. The proprietor of the factory is the son of Eli Whitney, who became eminent by the invention of the cotton-gin, a machine for separating the seed from the cotton, by which alone the culture of cotton could be extended. His invention was worth millions of dollars to the growers of cotton; but, like Fulton and other great inventors, he earned more honors than money; others reaped the benefit of his genius. He erected the manufactory of firearms which we now were visiting. The workmen had contributed twenty rifles for the Hungarian cause, and had expressed their desire to hand them personally to Kossuth. We saw them first engaged in their work, and then again passing before their guest and shaking hands with him. They all looked healthy, clean and intelligent. I was told that their wages amounted to from one and a half to four dollars a day.

Whilst the ceremony of welcome went on, I hastened with Mr. Pulszky to the houses where the workmen live. They are neat whitewashed buildings, one story high, surrounded by a garden, all of pretty equal size. We entered one, and found, on the ground-floor, a nice carpeted parlor. A piano stood at the wall, a round table in the midst of the room, several elegant chairs around, and various ornamental trinkets upon the mantel-piece. The upper story was occupied by three bed-rooms, each containing a large bed, a wash-stand, a table, a drawer and a couple of cane-chairs. *In all these rooms we noticed books.* I was curious to see what kind of literature interested the working classes here; I found the Bible, and instead of novels the life of the Virginian statesman, Patrick

Henry, travels, history, a translation of Ovid's Metamorphosis, and a heap of newspapers. We visited a second house; it was of the same description. We parted, with deep respect for a community where the workmen earn so much as to enjoy life with their families and to cultivate their minds. On our return, we were shown the grave of the two regicides, who under the Restoration had lived here in Connecticut, protected by the sympathies of the Colonists against the bloody decrees of Charles I.

After a most pleasant dinner with the cordial Mayor, we went on the railway to Springfield in Massachusetts. At Hartford, as on every station where the train stopped, enthusiastic crowds gathered round the cars. Kossuth addressed them with a few words....

POST-CIVIL WAR
CONNECTICUT

After the Civil War visitors to Connecticut, both native and foreign, had little choice but to acknowledge the extent to which industrialization was transforming the economy and culture of the state. But they did so in different ways.

In Samuel Adams Drake's case, the acknowledgment took the form of a denial. He confined his observations to areas of Connecticut that had been least transformed by industrialization at the time he wrote and focused on the dimensions of the past that had survived to the present. In Drake's account we see the ripening of a nostalgia for a vanishing pastoral world. An American, he appealed directly to those of his countrymen who reacted with aversion to the passing of traditional society.

By contrast, the Englishman Daniel Pidgeon, saw in Connecticut's expanding industrial enterprises nothing but good and gain. His account of the factories of the Naugatuck Valley read like descriptions of a new rational utopia which Connecticut had taken the lead in creating. Pidgeon perhaps had reason to be impressed with the native labor force's receptivity to technological innovation and the commitment of many upwardly aspiring operatives to sobriety, but he allowed his vision to be shaped unduly by the entrepreneurs who sponsored the industrial establishments he visited. He also undervalued the contributions non-English immigrants were making to the state's industrialization. Pidgeon, however, does reflect some of the ideological *élan* which the fruits of industrialism conferred on its proponents.

119

The other foreign observer from this period, and the only woman in the group, Agnes Watson, initially recorded her reactions to Connecticut for a private rather than a public audience. This gives her observations a candor which the other selections lack. Though her exposure to Connecticut was both brief in time and limited in extent, her letters nonetheless pinpoint the degree to which life in outlying towns like Glastonbury was being influenced by their proximity to cities such as Hartford and New York. By the end of the nineteenth century, transportation had improved to a point where someone could make the 150 mile journey either to or from New York in a long day. Going into Hartford to shop or sightsee was a routine event.

American visitors usually provided a better inventory than foreign ones did of what sights there were to see. Joel Cook supplies a comprehensive and integrated view of Connecticut as it approached the turn of the century. His glowing pictures of Bridgeport, New Haven, and Hartford convey his estimate of the state's success in achieving a balanced synthesis between the pastoral and industrial, between tradition and change. His account implies that in this respect Connecticut provided a model for the rest of the nation to emulate.

❦ SAMUEL ADAMS DRAKE ❧

Samuel Adams Drake was born in Boston, Massachusetts, in 1833, the son of Samuel and Louisa Drake. After attending public school in Boston, he married Isabella Mayhew in 1858 and moved to Kansas, working as a newspaper reporter and correspondent for papers back East. When the Civil War broke out, he joined the army and attained the rank of Brigadier-General in the Kansas Militia and Colonel in the Kansas Volunteers. In 1863 Isabella died. Three years later he returned to New England, where he married Olive Grant of Kennebunkport, Maine.

His father and brother Francis were historians, and it was not long before Samuel followed their lead and started writing on historical and related subjects. In the course of a busy writing career he produced twenty-five books in as many years. The account of Norwich, below, is from his Nooks and Corners of the New England Coast, *1875. He called one of his books an "historic-colloquial ramble," a characterization that fits much of his writing, although he did publish a number of regional histories—of New England, the West, and other sections of the United States.*

Drake was charmed by Norwich. The town, which rises step by step from the confluence of the Yantic and Shetucket rivers where they join to form the Thames, composes itself on its hillside into a view that has caught the eye of many artists. "Wherever one has made up his mind to be buried," Drake writes, "he would like to live in Norwich." Drake is among the visitors to Connecticut who have contributed to the state's continuing image as a pleasant place to live—small towns in country settings—an image that survives in novels and movies, and that continues to attract each evening an exodus of workers from New York City.

B. McN.

1875   New London is a city hiding within a river, three miles from its meeting with the waters of Long Island Sound. On the farthest seaward point of the western shore is a light-house. Before, and yet a little eastward of the river's mouth, is an island about nine miles long screening it from the full power of Atlantic storms, and forming, with Watch Hill, the prolongation of the broken line of land stretching out into the Sound from the northern limb of the Long Island shore. ...

Ascending now the river toward New London, wind, tide, or steam shall sweep us under the granite battlements of Fort Trumbull, on the

Excerpted from Samuel Adams Drake, *Nooks and Corners of the New England Coast*, New York, Harper, 1875.

one side, and the grassy mounds of Fort Griswold on the other. Near the latter is standing a monument commemorating the infamy of Benedict Arnold and the heroism of a handful of brave men sacrificed to what is called the chances of war.

New London is seen straggling up the side of a steep and rocky hill, dominated by three pointed steeples. Descending from the crest, its principal street opens like the mouth of a tunnel at the water-side into a broad space, always its marketplace and chief landing. Other avenues follow the natural shelf above the shore, or find their way deviously as streams might down the hill-side. The glory of New London is in its trees, though in some streets they stand so thick as to exclude the sun-light, and oppress the wayfarer with the feeling of walking in a churchyard. ...

Old London and Father Thames are repeated in New England, because, as these honest settlers avow, they loved the old names as much as they disliked the barbaric sounds of the aboriginal ones, though the latter were always typical of some salient characteristic. They settled upon the fair Mohegan, in the country of the Pequots, a race fierce and warlike, who in 1637 had made a death-grapple of it with the pale-faces, and had been blotted out from among the red nations. Pequot was the name of the harbor, changed in 1658 to New London. ...

All visitors to New London find their way, sooner or later, to the Old Hempstead House, a venerable roof dotted with moss-tufts, situated on Jay Street, not far west of the court-house. It is one of the few antiques which time and the flames have spared. As one of the old garrison-houses standing in the midst of a populous city, it is an eloquent reminder of the race it has outlived. It was built and occupied by Sir Robert Hempstead, descending as entailed property to the seventh generation, who continued to inhabit it. The Hempstead House is near the cove around which the first settlement of the town appears to have clustered. The last remaining house built by the first settlers stood about half a mile west of the court-house, on what was called Cape Ann Street: it was taken

"The glory of New London is in its trees..."   —*Samuel Adams Drake*

VIEW OF NEW LONDON, CONNECTICUT, FROM THE SHORE ROAD, BY H.B. WOOD.
ENGRAVING, 1854? (DETAIL)

down about 1824. Governor Winthrop lived at the head of the cove bearing his name at the north end of the city.

The court-house standing at the head of State (formerly Court) Street has the date of 1784 on the pediment, having been rebuilt after the burning of the town by Arnold. At the other end of the street was the jail. The court-house, which formerly had an exterior gallery, has a certain family resemblance to the State-house at Newport. It is built of wood, with some attempt at ornamentation. Freshened up with white paint and green blinds, it looked remarkably unlike a seat of justice, which is usually dirty enough in all its courts to be blind indeed.

In the chancel of St. James's repose the ashes of Samuel Seabury, the first Anglican bishop in the United States. He took orders in 1753 in London, and on returning to his native country entered upon the work of his ministry. In 1775, having subscribed to a royalist protest, declaring his "abhorrence of all unlawful congresses and committees," he was seized by the Whigs, and confined in New Haven jail. Later in the war, he bacame chaplain of Colonel Fanning's regiment of American loyalists. After the war, Mr. Seabury went to England in order to obtain consecration as bishop, but, meeting with obstacles there, he was consecrated in Scotland by three non-juring bishops....

The harbor of New London being considered one of the best in New England, its claim to be a naval station has been urged from time to time upon the General Government. It is spacious, safe, and deep. During the past winter, which has so severely tested the capabilities of our coast harbors, closing many of them with an ice-blockade of long continuance, that of New London has remained open. In 1835, when the navigation of the harbor of New York was suspended, by being solidly frozen, New London harbor remained unobstructed, vessels entering and departing as in summer. ...

With the aid of a wheezy ferryboat that landed me on Groton side, I still pursued my questionings or communings under the inspiration of a sunny afternoon, a transparent air, and a breeze brisk and bracing, bringing with it the full flavor of the sea. A climb up the step ascent leading to the old fort was rewarded by the most captivating views, and by gales that are above blowing in the superheated streets of a city.

The granite monument, which is our guide to the events these heights have witnessed, was built with the aid of a lottery. A marble tablet placed above its entrance is inscribed:

This Monument
was erected under the patronage of the
State of Connecticut, A.D. 1830,
and in the 55th year of the Independence of the U.S.A.,
In Memory of the Brave Patriots
who fell in the massacre of Fort Griswold, near this spot,
on the 6th of September, A.D. 1781,
When the British, under the command of the Traitor,
BENEDICT ARNOLD,
burnt the towns of New London and Groton, and spread
desolation and woe throughout this region.

Westminster Abbey could not blot out that arraignment. Dr. Johnson did not know Benedict Arnold when he said, "Patriotism is the last refuge of a scoundrel." An American school-boy, if asked to name the greatest villain the world has produced, would unhesitatingly reply, "The traitor, Benedict Arnold." The sentence which history has passed upon him is eternal. Some voice is always repeating it.

Shortly after the peace of '83 Arnold was presented at court. While the king was conversing with him, Earl Balcarras, who had fought with Burgoyne in America, was announced. The king introduced them.

"What, sire," exclaimed the haughty old earl, refusing his hand, "the traitor Arnold!"

The consequence was a challenge from Arnold. The parties met, and it was arranged they should fire together. Arnold fired at the signal, but the earl, flinging down his pistol, turned on his heel, and was walking away, when his adversary called out,

"Why don't you fire, my lord?"

"Sir," said the earl, looking over his shoulder, "I leave you to the executioner."...

With whatever local preferences the traveler may have come, he will think the approach to Norwich charming. Through banks high and green, crested with groves, or decked with white villages, the river slips quietly away to mingle in the noisy world of waters beyond. In deeper shadows of the hills the pictures along the banks are reproduced with marvelous fidelity of form and coloring; and even the blue of the sky and white drifting clouds are mirrored there. All terrestrial things, however, appear, as in the camera, inverted-roofs or steeples pointing downward, men or animals walking with feet upward, along the banks, like flies on a ceiling. When autumn tints are on, the effects seen in the water are heightened by the confused masses of sumptuous foliage hung like garlands along the shores.

Norwich is ranged about a hill overlooking the Thames. It is on a point of rock-land infolded by two streams, the Yantic and Shetucket, that come tumbling and hurrying down from the higher northern ranges to meet and kiss each other in the Thames. Rising, terrace above terrace, the appearance of Norwich, as viewed from the river, is more striking in its *ensemble* than by reason of particular features. The water-side is the familiar dull red, above which glancing roofs and steeples among trees are seen retreating up the ascent. By night a ridged and chimneyed blackness bestrewd with lights rewards the curious gazer from the deck of a Sound steamboat. I admired in Norwich the broad avenues, the wealth of old trees, the luxurious spaciousness of the private grounds. Washington Street is one of the finest I have walked in. There is breathing-room everywhere, town and country seeming to meet and clasp hands, each giving to the other of the best it had to offer. I do not mean that

Norwich is countrified; but its mid-city is so easily escaped as to do away with the feeling of imprisonment in a widerness of brick, stone, and plate-glass. The suburban homes of Norwich have an air of substantial comfort and delicious seclusion. In brief, wherever one has made up his mind to be buried, he would like to live in Norwich.

There are not a few picturesque objects about Norwich, especially by the shores of the Yantic, which, since being robbed of the falls, once its pride and glory, has become a prosaic mill-stream. The water is of the blackness of Acheron, streaked with amber where it falls over rocks, and of a rusty brown in shallows, as if partaking of the color of bits of decayed wood or dead leaves which one sees at the bottom. The stream, after having been vexed by dams and tossed about by mill-wheels, bounds joyously, and with some touch of savage freedom, to strike hands with the Shetucket.

The practical reader should be told that the city of Norwich is the outgrowth and was of yore the landing of Norwich town, two miles above it. The city was then known as Chelsea and Norwich Landing. The Mohegans were lawful owners of the soil. Subsequent to the Pequot war hostilities broke out between Uncas, chief of the Mohegans, and Miantonimo, the Narraganset sachem. The Narragansets invaded the territory of the Mohegans, and a battle occurred on the Great Plains, near Greenville, a mile and a half below Norwich. The Narrangansets suffered defeat, and their chief became a prisoner. He was delivered by Uncas to the English, who condemned him to death, and devolved upon Uncas the execution of the sentence. The captive chief was led to the spot where he had been made a prisoner, and, while stalking with Indian stoicism in the midst of his enemies, was killed by one blow from a tomahawk at the signal of Uncas. Miantonimo was buried where he fell, and from him the spot takes its name of Sachem's Plain.

War continued between the Narragansets and Mohegans, the former, led by a brother of Miantonimo, being again the assailants. Uncas was at length compelled to throw himself within his strong fortress, where he was closely besieged, and in danger of being overpowered. He found means to send intelligence to Saybrook, where Captain Mason commanded, that his supply of food was exhausted. Mason immediately sent Thomas Leffingwell with a boat-load of provision, which enabled Uncas to hold out until his enemy withdrew. For this act, which he performed single-handed, Leffingwell received from Uncas the greater part of Norwich; and in 1659, by a formal deed, signed by Uncas and his two sons, Owaneko and Attawanhood, he, with Mason, Rev. James Fitch, and others, became proprietors of the whole of Norwich.

I did not omit a visit to the ground where the "buried majesty" of Mohegan is lying. It is on the bank of the Yantic, in a secluded though populous neighborhood. A granite obelisk, with the name of Uncas in relief at its base, erected by citizens of Norwich, stands within the inclosure. The foundation was laid by President Jackson in 1833. Around are clustered a few mossy stones chiseled by English hands, with the brief record of the hereditary chieftains of a once powerful race. In its native state the spot must have been singularly romantic and well chosen. A wooded height overhangs the river in full view of the falls, where their turbulence subsides into a placid onward flow, and where the chiefs, ere their departure for the happy hunting-grounds, might look their last on the villages of their people. It was the Indian custom to bury by the margin of river, lake, or ocean. Here, doubtless, repose the bones of many grim warriors, seated in royal state, with their weapons and a pot of succotash beside them. The last interment here was of Ezekiel Mazeon, a descendant of Uncas, in 1826. The feeble remnant of the Mohegans followed him to the grave. ...

About midway of the pleasant avenue that unites old Norwich with new is the birthplace of Benedict Arnold. Somewhat farther on, and when within half a mile of the town, you also see at the right the homely little building which was the apothecary's in which Arnold worked as a boy with pestle and mortar to the acceptance of his master, Dr. Lathrop, who lived in the adjoining mansion. One can better imagine Arnold dealing out musket-bullets than pills, and mixing brimstone with salt-petre rather than harmless drugs. As a boy he was bold, high-spirited, and cruel.

In this neighborhood I saw a group of elms unmatched for beauty in New England. One of them is a king among trees. They are on a grassy slope, before an inviting mansion, and are in the full glory of maturity. It was a feast to stand under their branching arms, and be fanned and soothed by the play of the breeze among their green tresses, that fell in fountains of rustling foliage from their crowned heads. A benison on those old trees! May they never fall into the clutches of that class who have a real and active hatred of every thing beautiful, or that appeals to more than their habitual perception is able to discover...!

I had frequent opportunities of seeing, in my rambles about the environs of New London and Norwich, the beautiful dwarf flowering laurel *(Kalmia augustifolia)* that is almost unknown farther north. In the woods, where it was growing in wild luxuriance, it appeared like a gigantic azelia, ablaze with fragrant bloom of white and pink. It used to be said that honey collected by the bee from this flower was poisonous. The broad-leaved laurel, or calico-tree *(Kalmia latifolia)* was believed to be even more injurious, instances being mentioned where death had occurred from eating the flesh of pheasants that had fed on its leaves.

Norwich town represents the kernel from which the city has sprung, and retains also no little of the savor incident to a population that has held innovations at arms-length. It has quiet, freshness, and a certain rural comeliness. A broad green, or common, planted with trees, is skirted by houses, many of them a century or more old, among which I thought I now and then detected the no longer familiar well-sweep, with the "old oaken bucket" standing by the curb. On one side of the common the old court-house is still seen.

Take the path beside the meeting-house, ascending the overhanging rocks by some natural steps, and you will be richly repaid for the trifling exertion. The view embraces a charming little valley watered by the Yantic, which here flows through rich meadow-lands and productive farms. Encompassing the settlement is another elevated range of the rocky hills common to this region, making a sort of amphitheatre in which the town is naturally placed.

The old church of Norwich town formerly stood in the hollow between two high hills above its present site. ... I visited the old grave-yard, remarkable for its near return to a state of nature. Many stones had fallen, and sometimes two were kept upright by leaning one against the other. Weeds, brambles, and vines impeded my footsteps or concealed the grave-stones. I must often repeat the story of the shameful neglect which involves most of our older cemeteries. One is not quite sure, in leaving them, that he does not carry away on his feet the dust of former generations. Some of the stones are the most curious in form and design I have met with. The family tombs of Governor and General Huntington are here.

ঌ DANIEL PIDGEON ঌ

*L*ittle *is known about Daniel Pidgeon, an English engineer, beyond the abbreviations on the title page his book,* Old-World Questions and New-World Answers, *(1884) identifying him as a Fellow of the Geographical Society and an associate instructor of civil engineering. This book, supplementing one published the year before titled* An Engineer's Holiday; or, Notes of a Round Trip from Long. 0° to 0°, *was described at the time of publication as "a record written with spirit, humour, and singularly keen observation, of a rambling tour among the manufacturing towns and villages of New England." In observing the industrial centers of Connecticut, Pidgeon's trained eye provides a unique picture of the social history of factory towns as well as manufacturing processes. He viewed America as "a great alembic," an appa-*

ratus that refines or transmutes by distillation, and was fascinated by the action that would convert the raw material from Europe into "the American people that is yet to be." Continuing his scientific analogy, Pidgeon called democracy a social solvent and public education a crystallizing agent in the Americanization process. Europeans, he felt, could learn a great deal by watching the new world closely.

Pidgeon's first stop in the Connecticut portion of his tour was Ansonia where he visited pin and telegraph wire factories. Chapter III describes "Clockland," whose capital is Waterbury and Chapter IV, "Winsted - A Temperance Town." Most of the omitted passages in the following excerpt are comprised of his detailed reports on factory operations and town histories.

J. S.

1883 It was a bright May morning, with the sky of Italy and air more invigorating than wine, when we started, an Anglo-American party of two, with the intention of visiting some of the Naugatuck and Housatonic factories, and of seeing how the homes of labour in New England differ from those of Old England. Leaving New York, the railway skirts the coast and crosses a seemingly endless succession of drift beds, plainly of glacial origin. The drift overlies azoic gneisses, huge shoulders of which rise above a plain of arable soil, just as islands rise from a sea. Where the primitive rock is very thinly covered with earth, there occur patches of forest trees, whose roots scarcely find sustenance in the crevices to which they cling. Saving the forest, the aspect of the country is essentially English. Small fields are divided from one another by walls built of the boulders picked from the soil. Pretty farmhouses recur at short intervals and snug private houses, surrounded by well-kept gardens, herald, now and again, our approach to flourishing towns.

Arrived at Stratford, where the Housatonic debouches into the Sound, we strike northwards and follow the river to its junction with

Excerpted from Daniel Pidgeon, *Old-World Questions and New-World Answers*, London, Kegan Paul, Trench & Co., 1884.

the Naugatuck, through a country, also of rounded gneissic hills, which are deeply buried in level sheets of drift. Clearings and forest alternate for a time, but the latter presently prevails. Tiny brooks of clear brown water wander around the stems of the trees and among the mossy bosses of rock, while great tufts of the "skunk cabbage" *(Symplocarpus foetidus)* spring abundantly beside every watercourse, arresting attention by their brilliant green colour. "New England is a country of laughing brooks," said a travelling companion once to Mr. Secretary Evarts, who was as great a joker as he was a good lawyer. "It must be so," was the answer, "or the books would not say so much about 'diverting watercourses.'"

The Housatonic and Naugatuck join at Derby, where their united streams sweep majestically around high hills which are everywhere covered with forest, leafless and grey as yet, but relieved by occasional clumps of beautiful evergreen hemlocks. Entering the Naugatuck valley, we caught sight of the manufacturing town of Birmingham, lying on the junction of the two streams. The name recalls ideas of a smoky town, with dingy suburbs, overhung by a murky sky, but the view from our car windows was of something very different from this. A number of massive brick buildings—one scarcely knew in the distance whether they were factories or castles—lined the beautiful curve of the river, and shone, rosy red, in the sunlight, though pearly morning mist. Above the latter, which lay low on the water, rose tier upon tier of gleaming white houses, the highest of them peeping out from the hillside forest, whilst overhead was the blue arch of an Italian sky.

The Naugatuck river is a clear mountain stream of considerable volume, which, but for the intervention of man, would seek the sea in a series of rapids. It has, however, been so often dammed as to exhibit a succession of beautiful mountain tarns, whence artificial canals, called "raceways," lead to the various mills. We made our first halt at Ansonia, the creation and namesake of a Mr. Anson Platt, who dammed the river at this spot about thirty years ago, and built the first

"...massive brick buildings - one scarcely knew in the distance whether they were factories or castles..."

—*Daniel Pidgeon*

Works of the Scovill Manufacturing Company, Waterury, Conn, anonymous. Wood engraving, n.d. (detail)

of the great "brass-mills" for which the Naugatuck is now famous. These mills all originated in the following way. The stream, being easily controllable, while its flow of water is abundant, offered great advantages to the early makers of wooden clocks, who may be called the pioneers of manufacture in America. They established small water-wheels and modest workshops here in considerable numbers and, by-and-by, as metal came into use for clock-making, a few brass-rolling and wire-drawing mills arose in the valley. These, when the staple trade was dull, sought an outlet for their sheet and wire by making pins, lamp-fittings, cartridges, ferrules, arrow-heads, shoe-tips, corset studs, wire chain, and a thousand other trifles, such as can be stamped from brass sheet or twisted out of wire. There came a brief, bright time, indeed, when every mill on the Naugatuck turned its attention with advantage to the making of "hoop-skirts." But when fashion presently decreed the reign of scanty dresses, an industrial earthquake shook the crinoline factories almost to their foundations. Since then clocks and pins have dominated the district and, if I say nothing of the former until we reach Waterbury, the capital of Clockland, the latter may be appropriately sung at Ansonia.

There were but two pinmakers in the American colonies during revolutionary times, viz. Jeremiah Wilkinson, a Rhode Island wire-drawer, and Samuel Slocum, also of Rhode Island, whose patent machine for making solid-headed pins was already working in England. At this time, imported pins sold for 7s. 6d. a dozen; so that we read without surprise of a State offer of "£50 for the best twenty-five dozen pins of domestic make, equal to those imported from England. In 1831, Dr. Howe, of New York, invented a machine which made pins at one operation, and, a few years later, a pinmaking company was formed, which continued its operations, under the charge of Dr. Howe, until 1865.

The Wallace Brass-Mill, one of the largest concerns in Ansonia, owes its origin to the introduction of the Howe pin-machine. This has already created a demand for brass wire, which could not be met, except by importation, there being little practical skill in wire drawing available in America at that time, when Mr. Wallace, originally an English wire-drawer, was found working at Birmingham, Connecticut, and proved the man for the occasion. He was soon persuaded to pitch his tent at Ansonia, and began making pinwire about twenty-five years ago, with scarcely twenty men to assist him. His mills now employ seven hundred hands, and, aside from wire and sheet, turn out enormous quantities of the useful trifles, of which some have already been enumerated. These, like pins, are all produced by extremely clever and very interesting automatic machinery, which it seems the special province of the Americans, and especially of the Connecticut mechanic, to devise.

134

This remarkable character, who, more than any other person or circumstance, has given its distinctive features to American manufacture, is a figure of so much industrial importance that we cannot make his acquaintance one moment too soon. He is usually a Yankee of Yankees by birth and of a temperament thoughtful to dreaminess. His natural bent is strongly towards mechanical pursuits, and he finds his way, very early in life, into the workshop. Impatient of the fetters which trade societies forge for less independent minds, he delights to make his own bargain with his employer, and, whatever be the work on which he is engaged, bends the whole force of an acute but narrow intelligence to scheming means for accomplishing it easily. Unlike the English mechanic, whom a different education and different circumstances have taught to believe his own interest ill served by facilitating the operations of the workshop, the Connecticut man is profoundly convinced to the contrary. He cherishes a fixed idea of creating a monopoly in some branch of manufacture, by establishing an overwhelming superiority over the methods of production already existing in that branch. To "get up" a machine, or series of machines, for this purpose, is his one aim and ambition. If he succeeds, supported by patents and the ready aid which capital gives to promising novelty in the States, he may revolutionize an industry, forcing opponents, who produce in the old way, altogether out of the market, while benefiting the consumer and making his own fortune at the same time.

The workshops of Massachusetts, Rhode Island, and, especially, of Connecticut, are full of such men. Usually tall, thin, reflective, and taciturn, but clever and, above all things, free, the equals, although mechanics, of the capitalist upon whose ready alliance they can count, they are an element of incalculable value to American industry. Their method of attacking manufacturing problems is one which, intelligently handled, must command markets by simultaneously improving qualitites and cheapening prices. We ourselves certainly aim, as they do, at the specialization of manufacture, but one scarcely treads upon the threshold of Clockland before feeling how much more universally the system

135

is being applied in the States than here. Tools and processes which we are inclined to consider as exceptionally clever are the commonplaces of American shops, and the determination to do nothing by hand which can be done by a machine is a marked characteristic of the work-man there, while it scarcely exists among operatives here. The "Connecticut man" will crop up again and again in the course of our trip. He is an element of the utmost importance in the industrial develop-ment of America, a force of which we, unfortunately, have no equiva-lent in England, and that is why I have taken the earliest opportunity of introducing him to the reader.

Returning to pins, it is really charming, if I may use a word usually reserved for descriptions of personal or natural beauty, to watch the pretty little automaton called a pin-machine. This little creature feeds heartily, but without haste, on a coil of brass wire and, immediately after taking a bite, turns one end of the pin that is to be, held firmly in a grip-ping die, towards a small hammer, whose blows fall too rapidly to be counted or even seen. The headed shanks next drop, one by one, into radial notches in a horizontal disc, where they look like pointless pins stuck, heads inward, around a flat pin-cushion. This pin-cushion turns slowly round, and pre-sents each projecting shank successively to the rims of three tiny grindstones, revolving at a very high speed, which first form and then finely finish the points. Hour by hour the steel jaws snip the wire, the hammers beat their rapid tattoo on the heads, the rowel of wire shanks turns slowly over the hissing little grindstones, discharging a hundred and seventy finished pins per minute. It is like watching, through a micro-scope, the wheel-like play of a rotifer's cilia.

Time and the reader's patience would both fail, did I attempt to describe all the automata of the Wallace Brass-Mill. Here is a row of strange organ-isms, in shining nickel-plate costumes, nipping away, like the pin-machine, at a roll of brass wire, and carrying the pieces, one at a time, by means of fingers as shapely as those of a girl, to be headed, and then dropping them, finished corset studs, as fast as one can count, into a box. There is another group of wire-eaters, taking in brass and turning out chain at the rate of seventy links a minute, no one regarding, while the links grow from yards to miles. Here is a wonderful automaton which sticks two thousand pins a minute into pin-papers and, there, another which punches, folds, and glues together cardboard pin-boxes, at the rate of a thousand an hour. Such is the character of the surroundings among which the Connecticut man lives, moves, and has his being. Here he observes, alters, amends and schemes. These pulsating and quasi-living beings are his children and companions, who give him occupation, pleasure and stimulation. The thousand wants of the world offer him a boundless field for his creative powers, and, silently brooding, he brings forth, now and again, a new automaton, as a poet produces a verse, or a musician a melody.

The deep, thrilling notes of many steam-whistles having proclaimed the factory dinner-hour, we made our way, in company with a stream of artisans of both sexes, to the "Hodgkiss House," in search of refreshment. Married operatives in America usually live in their own houses, while unmarried labour generally "rooms" in tenement houses and "boards" in establishments, which, while practically eating-houses, are ostensibly hotels. "Table boarders" are sometimes called simply "mealers," or even, when a buggy goes round to collect the scattered *clientèle* of a given house, "hauled mealers;" but we, on this occasion, were "transient mealers."

We entered a large dining-room, very clean, well furnished, and simply but nicely decorated, set with small, separate tables, dressed in the whitest linen and attended by trim girls, who, if their manners were independent, waited smilingly and well. No printed bill of fare appeared, but the waitress whispered rapidly in the ear of each guest, "Hash and tea, pork and beans, potatoes, stringbeans, succotash, pie-plant pie, apple and cranberry pie." A little puzzled, but always anxious to act the Roman in Rome, I called for "Hash and tea, succotash, and pie-plant pie;" and then looked around at the company. The room was crowded with diners of both sexes, whose dress, manners, and speech scarcely distinguished them from an average hotel crowd and, hampered as yet by English ideas, I had to ask more than once if I was really among American artisans. Before I could feel fully assured on this point, came my hash and tea; I dared not ask for beer, for, likely enough, Ansonia might be a teetotal town, and I already knew that American operatives drink nothing stronger than ice-water, coffee, and tea. The compound of beef and potatoes was excellent, and "succotash" proved to be a stew of mixed Indian corn and beans, a dish which, as I afterwards learned, the Pilgrim Fathers adopted from the natives. "Pie-plant pie" was a surprise, being nothing else than rhubarb tart, predestinarian Puritanism having early recognized and acknowledged by name the manifest destiny of this useful vegetable. The midday meal was soon despatched, the orderly, respectable crowd strolled off to the various factories, and we found ourselves, after a temperate repast, fit for any amount more work, while the day was as yet hardly half-spent. ...

Ascending the Naugatuck valley for a few miles, we reached Waterbury, a town of twenty thousand inhabitants and the capital of Clockland, where, within a radius of twenty miles, more clocks are made than in any other part of the world. There is, indeed, a hint, in the scenery of Naugatuck, of that other watch country, Switzerland, whose industrious people till their ungrateful mountain farms in summer and make watches in their chalets during winter. Here is the same rough country and poor farming land, but the people are congregated in great factories, where thousands of clocks are made every day, by means of beautiful special machinery.

Fifty years ago, a clock was an heirloom, even in well-to-do American families, but scarcely any home is without one to-day, and this change has been brought about by the skill and enterprise of the Connecticut man. Towards the close of the last century Eli Terry established himself in the town of Plymouth, Connecticut, and began making wooden clocks. The teeth of the wheels were first described by a pair of compasses and then cut out with a handsaw, while, aside from a few pivots and fastenings, there was not a piece of metal in the old Yankee clocks. For a good many years, Terry sold his clock movements for five pounds apiece and these were cased by the local joiner whenever the farmer or trader brought one home to his family and village. That is why the upright clocks of a hundred years ago have so much character about them and the true reason of their popularity among persons of good taste. In 1807, Terry commenced making wooden clocks by machinery and, about the same time, Riley Whiting, another Connecticut man, started a wooden-clock factory at Winsted, a few miles from Waterbury. He introduced a great many improvements in the manufacture and finally became the most important clockmaker of his day in America.

Meanwhile, competition had already reduced the price of wooden movements from five pounds to twenty shillings, when a certain Chauncey Jerome suddenly revolutionized Clockland, by the introduction of a clock made entirely of brass. The framework and wheels of this timepiece were punched out of sheet metal and its spindles turned in automatic lathes, the effect of this change in the common practice being to reduce the cost of a clock movement to about two shillings and the price of cased clocks to eight or ten shillings apiece. A first consignment of Connecticut clocks was sent to England in 1842 and, since that time, not only have they found their way into almost every British kitchen and cottage, but have been scattered by millions broadcast over the whole world. ...

Clockmaking, as we have seen, was an important industry in the Naugatuck valley before watchmaking by machinery had come to the birth, but it was not in the nature of the Connecticut man to be satisfied with [limited success.] He burned to do for watches what Chauncey Jerome had done for clocks; to make them by the million, for the million and put them into everybody's pocket, as clocks had already been put upon everybody's mantelpiece. We shall see how far he has succeeded, when, after a glance at the works of the Waterbury Clock Company, we find our way to the splendid factory of the Waterbury Watch Company, scarcely as yet five years old, but one of the most beautiful industrial establishments in the world. ...

The Waterbury Clock Company's factory is a veritable palace of industry. The building is dignified, if not handsome, in appearance and, as usual in America, specially designed for the purpose to which it is applied. It is spacious enough for the future extension of business, convenient for work and comfortable in all its arrangements, both for master and man.

The New England manufacturer has no notion of spending the greater part of his day in a dirty, ill-furnished, ill-ventilated room, or, indeed, of asking his book-keepers to do so. On the contrary, he houses his staff in large, handsome rooms, fitted with many clever devices for facilitating work, from among which the telephone is never absent. Most of his clerks are girls, who also conduct the correspondence, using the type-writer almost universally for this purpose. The offices are kept scrupulously neat and clean and their occupants are distinguished by an air of briskness very different to that which characterizes their duller brethren of the desk in England. The workshops, again, are so comfortable, and the operatives so like the masters in ideas and manners, that an Englishman is altogether, but very agreeably, surprised on his first introduction to a Yankee factory....

The roots of our civilization were laid in feudality, although they have branched into freedom, but the tree has yet to bear the flower of equality. Hence, we remain a race of castes, whose boundary lines are so rigid as to be, at present, impassable. The "upper" and "lower" strata of society, the idle and industrial classes, indeed, cannot amalgamate, for they are separated by differences so profound that contact between them must be attended either by servility or hostility. Centuries of inequality have so degraded labour that its ranks are now effectually barred to culture, and our golden youth is squandered while we wait for the renascence of industry.

Matters are very different in New England. The owners of these brass-mills and clock-shops are proud of that industry which—not only with their lips, but by their lives—they honour. Their operatives, with whom one dines at every Hodgkiss House in the Naugatuck valley, are well educated, well mannered and intelligent companions, hopeful as to their own chances of success in life, satisfied to see cleverer men than themselves growing rich and honouring industry, because they, the children of industry, are honoured.

But I am moralizing outside the factory, while my readers are anxious to go within. Having passed through the cheerful offices and admired the trim girl-clerks, our attention is pointedly drawn to a new system of fire-prevention, now coming into use throughout manufacturing New England. These mountain towns are well supplied with water, whose pressure is high and supply constant. A network of pipes, in connection with the town mains, is fixed to every ceiling in the factory, the pipes themselves being furnished with "sprinklers," or roses, each of which commands a space of about ten feet square. The plugs are closed by fusible metal, which melts at a temperature of a hundred and fifty degrees, giving vent, in case of danger, to a rush of water sufficient to extinguish any incipient fire. As a concurrent effect of any one of these plugs melting, an alarm-bell is set violently ringing, the whole arrangement being perfectly automatic and always ready for action. ...The Waterbury Clock Company make about fifteen hundred clocks a day, and the total production of the New England clock-shops is not less than ten thousand a day. These are sold at prices varying from five shillings to ten pounds a piece, and are sent to every part of the world.

If the Waterbury Clock Company's factory is properly called a palace of industry, I want a new name to characterize that of the Waterbury Watch Company. The building itself looks like a fine town hall or museum and we, indeed, entered its handsome vestibule, doubtful whether we had not mistaken some public instituition for a manufactory. But we were soon reassured on this point by the manager,

Mr. Lock, who responded to our letters of introduction with customary American kindness.

The watch factories of Massachusetts, whose origin and history have
already been sketched, had long made it easy for people of moderate
means to carry the time in their pockets, when it occured to some of the
long-sighted manufacturers of the Naugatuck valley that a good, reli-
able watch, at a price of about three dollars, would find a wide, unoc-
cupied field and might pay. The cheapest Waltham watch, constructed
of more than a hundred and sixty pieces, costs a great deal more than
three dollars, and the first thing therefore required to carry out the proposed programme was a good time-keeper, no toy, which should have
fewer pieces in it than any existing watch.

There came, one day, a Massachusetts watch-repairer into the
Centennial Exhibition, with a steam-engine in his waistcoat pocket, which,
although a thimble covered it, had a boiler, cylinder, piston, valves, governor, crank and crank shaft, and would work. The maker, Mr. Buck,
placed it side by side with the great Corliss engine, which was one of
the wonders of the Philadelphia show and, thus juxtaposed, these representatives of dignity and impudence remained throughout the exhibition. Mr. Charles Benedict, a partner in one of the largest brass-mills
on the Naugatuck and one of the promoters of the cheap watch scheme,
saw it, and, presently, asked Mr. Buck to design the three-dollar watch
of the future. He undertook the commission, and, at first, failed. But
a Yankee inventor follows a mechanical trail with the perseverance of
an Indian and, within a year, the watch-hunter had made a practical timepiece, having only fifty-eight pieces in it, all told. He took it to Mr. Benedict,
who tested it in every possible way and the watch stood the tests.

Preparations were at once commenced to make it on a large scale. A
factory, designed by Hartwell, the architect of Waltham, was erected, and
two years were spent in filling it with the necessary tools and machinery. Although the watch was to be cheap, it did not follow that the plant
for producing it should be cheap also, and so it happened that, when the

building was finished and furnished, nearly half a million of dollars had been expended. Manufacturing operations were commenced in May, 1881, and since that date the "Waterbury Watch," as it was called, has been steadily produced at the rate of six hundred a day, or one per minute.

All the parts of this watch are interchangeable. If you had a pint each of wheels, pinions, springs and pivots, you could put any of them together and the watch so produced would go and keep time. That is because each piece is made by automatic machinery, which cannot make errors as the hand can. But if you took twenty Swiss watches to pieces and shuffled up their parts, you would spoil twenty watches, and not be able to make one that would go without fitting.

Having told us all this and much more, Mr. Lock put us in charge of a guide and we made a circuit of the workshops. These might more appropriately be called saloons, so sightly are they and so beautifully fitted with every appliance for comfort and convenience. Entering at the operatives' door, we came, first, upon the dressing-room, where each workman has his ticketed hooks for coat, and hat, his own ticketed towel, while the common lavatory is equal to that of an English club. The girls' toilet-room is quite dainty in its arrangements, a separate supply of water, for instance, and separate vessels for face and hand washing being provided. The most exact neatness and scrupulous cleanliness are ensured, by the appointment of a special attendant to this usually neglected department.

The "train-room" and "assembly-room" constitute the bulk of the factory and to these everything else is ancillary. The first requisites of a watch factory are abundance of light, neatness, and cleanliness. No man can do his best when physically uncomfortable, whether from excess of heat or cold, a poor light, or, above all, bad air. It is now universally acknowledged, at least in the Naugatuck valley, that everything which contributes to the physical comfort and mental benefit of the workman pays a good return on its first cost. Hence, the walls of the train-room are all windows, the ceilings are high, the warming and ventilation is perfect. There is no smoke, dust, or bad air, and the operatives are comfortably seated at their respective benches.

The beautiful and costly special machinery which aids watch-making, as carried on in the States, is collected in this apartment. Here the various wheels, pinions, and pivots, forming the "train" of a watch, are made, the little automata which produce them being watched and tended, one cannot say directed, by girls. Here, for example, is the self-acting wheel-cutter, which spaces and cuts the teeth of fifty wheels at once. All its attendant has to do is to pick up fifty blanks, just as they come from the stamping department, slip them on a spindle, offer this to the automaton, cover the latter with a metal shield, to keep out dust, and start the machine. This, then, goes soberly on, feeding the wheels up to the cutters and spacing the teeth until all are cut, when it stops. The finished wheels are taken out, new blanks are supplied and the wheel-cutter resumes work. There, again, is an automatic "staff"-turning lathe. The bit of steel wire on which it operates is only a tenth of an inch in diameter and a quarter of an inch long, but requires twenty-seven distinct operations to shape it to the proper form and dimensions. The girl who tends this machine really superintends some sixteen thousand movements a day, sitting at her ease meanwhile in a comfortable chair, and giving her charge an occasional drop of oil.

The "assembly-room" might justify its name if it were a question of a county ball, instead of watchmaking. Here, the parts we have watched in the making are given out, by the pint and the pound, and grow into movements, under the deft fingers of a number of specially trained watch-makers, at the rate of one per minute. Then they are cased and, lastly, placed in shallow trays, holding each about three hundred watches, for testing. The trays are supported upon pivots, and can be swung into any position between the vertical and horizontal. The watches remain first upright, then at an angle of 45° and, finally, upside down; for a space of six days altogether, going all the time. Those which stop, or fail to keep time, are sent back to the "assembly-room," while those which pass muster are boxed and despatched to the native and foreign markets.

This factory cost, as we have seen, about half a million of dollars, employs three hundred hands and turns out six hundred watches a day. These sell for two dollars forty-three cents a piece, and if any one should ask Mr. Lock, "Why not for an even two-fifty?" he might perhaps answer, as once before, to such an inquirer, "Don't you know? Three cents is the cost of the watch, the *profit* is an even two-forty."

A few moments before six o'clock, we stationed ourselves at the factory door to watch the issuing operatives. Of these, the greater number are girls, but, girl or man, almost every one had a smile and a nod for the manager, a smile and nod which were charming because of their eloquence as to the relations between employer and employed. Of one, Mr. Lock would say, "He is our librarian;" of another, "He teaches in my Sunday school; of this girl, "She is the best singer in our church choir;" of that, "She is my wife's right hand at a bee." If there is military discipline inside the works, there is both friendship and equality between employer and employed without its walls. When Jack is really as good as his master, the old proverb has no sting.

The Naugatuck valley heads about thirty miles north of Waterbury and as our train threads its rocky bed, sweeps around its frequent curves and enters its open bottoms, or "intervales," as they are here called, we find the last almost always occupied by industrial towns. These are seldom more than three or four miles apart, are all Ansonias or Waterburys in appearance, full of brass-mills, clock-shops, pin factories and similar establishments.

Arrived within ten miles of the river's source, where it is no longer able to turn a mill-wheel, the railway leaves the stream and, crossing a low divide, reaches, within a few miles, another mountain stream, called the Mad River. This is small but turbulent tributary of the Farmington, a river of considerable industrial importance, which drives a thousand wheels in its long, tortuous course through hills that turn it, now north, now south, on its way to join the Connecticut river. The Mad River valley is the double of the Naugatuck, excavated in the same primitive rocks and bordered by similar deposits of glacial *detritus*. These have been stratified by the action of water, and are conspicuous by their arrangement into flanking terraces, upon whose level, continuous surfaces the railways of these New England glens seek their remotest water powers, as if by ready-made roads.

The woods on either side of the valley began to show signs of the coming spring. Although the birches and chestnuts were still quite bare, the half-unfolded leaves of some early maples patched the dark hemlocks with crimson, while the bloom of an occasional dogwood shone like a snowball against groves of evergreen pine. The river brawled loudly over its steep rocky bed and the air grew keen as we rose from the lower valley towns to a level of about seven hundred feet above the sea.

Here lies Winsted, a half-agricultural, half-mechanical town, of six thousand souls, jammed in a rocky glen, which is only just wide enough to accommodate its main street. This curves around a wide bend in the noisy stream, beside which it straggles for a long way, a broken line of churches, factories, stores and private houses. Cross streets branch from it irregularly, ascending lateral valleys which lose themselves in grassy uplands and spread the dwellings of a few thousand people over the area of a little city.

They have an odd way in Connecticut of giving compound names to such new places as grow up from time to time between two or more existing townships in the State. Winsted is a case in point. It lies on the borders of Winchester and Berkhampstead, and has therefore been called Winsted. Waterbury itself is a compound of Watertown and Middlebury, Torringford of Torrington and Hartford, and Wintonbury of Windsor Farmington and Simsbury. The custom is fruitful of names having a sound which is English in character without being familiar to the ear. ...

... Indian pudding? Well, that is a kind of fritter made of maize flour, a dish which, in old colonial days, was eaten boiled on Saturday, while what remained "the queen next day had fried." These fine distinctions of right and wrong are not confined to New England. I remember, when a boy, that the Sunday dinner of cold meat was, indeed, relieved by boiled potatoes, but "it was wrong" to cook anything else. In the same way, baked potatoes were an orthodox dish for Sunday's supper, in families where it would have been thought sinful to grill a steak or toast a Welsh rarebit. They were not too good to boil and bake for us on the sabbath at Winsted, but the man must be an infidel or an agnostic who breakfasts without Indian pudding on the Lord's day in New England.

The village streets were as silent as the grave when we sallied out of the hotel for a morning walk. The white wooden houses, with their green jalousies, looked prim and prudish, while a most uncompromising church dominated the silent streets with a stark wooden spire. Presently, a stream of young people of both sexes, neat in dress and proper in manner, filed this way and that to their respective Sunday schools. At nine o'clock precisely, the church bell began to ring, not for the assembly of worshippers, but a "warning peal." This, in the colonial days, when a clock, as we have seen, was an heirloom, told the outlying farmers it was time to hitch up their teams and start with their families for the meeting-house. The bell still continues to toll, although every rural mantelpiece is now furnished with its two-dollar timepiece. ...

We strolled upwards from the main street towards the grassy slopes which surround the town, admiring the beautiful foliage of the hemlocks and wondering at the number of cottages which we saw in course of erection. The artisans of New England live, much more commonly than those of Old England, in their own houses. ...

Building is certainly made easy for operatives in New England. At Winsted, Mr. Gilbert, one of the largest clock-masters in the district, puts up houses for any of his men at the rate of seven hundred dollars, or £140, for house and lot, a hundred dollars being paid down and the balance standing on easy terms of interest and repayment. Mr. Gilbert is a rich man, who likes this kind of investment, but his practice only gives effect to the principles of New England manufacturers generally. They are convinced that the magic of property makes men at once better citizens and more valuable servants. Hence, where there are no Gilberts, the banks take their places and no steady operative finds it difficult to build a house, while many of them do so without borrowing money. These artisans' dwellings are not only roomy and comfortable, but very attractive in appearance. They have basements of cut stone, surmounted by a tasteful superstructure of wood, a wide verandah, kitchen, parlour and bedroom on the ground floor and three bedrooms above, besides cupboards and pantries. They are always painted white and adorned with green jalousies, both these features being as much *de rigueur* as Indian pudding for sabbath day's breakfast. When these pretty homes, with their clean faces, well-tilled quarter-acre lots and windows aglow with geraniums, are scattered, as in the Mad River and Naugatuck valleys, amid beautiful mountainglens, they suggest that American labour lives in an atmosphere characterized by something which is more than comfort if less than culture. It is time, indeed, to step within doors and see how the Connecticut artisan, whose acquaintance we have already made in the workshop, appears *chez lui*.

Our friend Mr. S— is an Ansonia mechanic who occupies the ground floor of his own house, which is considerably larger than the single houses already described, and lets the upper part to a fellow operative. His pretty cottage looks, upwards, to the wooded slopes of the Green Mountain range; downwards, upon the river Naugatuck, with its blue lake-like millponds and surrounding factories, from whose distant chimneys arises nothing worse than white puffs of steam. We found his wife and daughter reading on the verandah, and were welcomed by them with a manner charmingly compounded of simplicity, independence and the wish to please. Within, was a pleasant sitting-room, furnished with all the comforts and some of the luxuries of life. The tables were strewn with books. For musical instruments there was the American organ, while some pretty photographs adorned the walls. No refreshment was offered us, for they drink nothing in temperate New England and no one eats between the regular meal hours. ...

Like many other freeholders of the same class, Mr. S— lets one-half his house and lives in the other, his tenant being a German-American mechanic, whose wife only was at home when we called. Well, indeed, does this bright little woman deserve her name of Rosenbaum, for she lives surrounded by flowers, of which she is an ardent lover and successful cultivator. Roses and geraniums crowded every corner of Mrs. Rosenbaum's room, so that our talk fell naturally on her hobby, which she discussed with great enthusiasm and many smiles. Although the same people, we were no longer the same party as when below stairs. A gleam of continental brightness shone from the cheery German frau over Yankee seriousness and English phlegm. Her national character had gained independence from American associations, without losing its lighter, pleasure-loving traits. A family of six children lived on this modest flat; but they had all evidently been trained in habits of extreme neatness, for every room, from kitchen to attic, was spotlessly clean and in apple-pie order.

Such are the homes of native American labour and of those foreign workmen who have lived for a long time under native American influences. We shall hereafter find, among immigrant artisans, dwellings and tenants corresponding much more closely than do these to our notions of workmen and workmen's homes. Already, indeed, we foresee that important questions, as to the reciprocal influence of European labour and American ideas, will arise as we proceed, but these we are not yet in a position to discuss. For the present we are content to note that the wave of emigration which has already flooded many American industries, especially the textiles, has not yet risen to great heights in Clockland. There, as in the boot and shoe factories of Massachusetts, the operatives are still, for the most part, genuine Yankees, although their numbers are constantly being diminished by the attractions which the Far West offers to enterprising natures. ...

We were late in returning to our hotel for midday dinner, and this, a grave fault on week-days, is, on Sundays, a crime which, if not openly reprimanded, demands some sort of rebuke. Household "help" in America is quite as independent as any other form of labour, and a girl who has bargained, either to cook or to wait at table during certain hours of the day, resents the tarrying of guests as a breach of contract. Hence, a certain acidity in our prim waitress' tone when reciting the simple ménu, and a notable increase in the velocity with which the young lady usually slung us our food. We took our punishment penitently, however, for the girl, if petulant, was pretty; but we dared not offer any one of those propitiatory little attentions which would have made an English maid kind to worse culprits than we.

Although the sale of alcoholic liquors is lawful in every State of New England except Maine, "local option" forbids the drink traffic in many towns, and this is the case at Winsted. The Maine liquor law is frequently spoken of in England as if it were peculiar to that State, and is sometimes accused of promoting habits of secret drinking. The first idea is a mistaken one, as the case of Winsted proves, while the baselessness of the second supposition is best understood by mixing with the operatives of New England generally. They, although rarely professed teetotallers, are universally abstainers. Beer is never seen on the tables of the houses where they board, or drunk in their own homes. The public-house is hard to find in many New England towns where the sale of liquor is not forbidden, the bar-loafer is a rarity, and it is quite impossible to meet the slattern, so common in our own streets, carrying home her jug of "eleven o'clock."

The voters for "no liquor" are, usually, themselves working men. It is the clock-makers, the scythe-grinders, the axle-smiths and the silk-spinners of Winsted who have closed the public-house, but American mill-owners, storekeepers and farmers are almost unanimously in favour of the temperance ticket and hold "rum towns" in horror. American operatives are advocates of temperance for a reason which is, unfortunately, of little applicability in Europe. None of them begin life with the expectation of being always mere labourers. All intend to possess a comfortable degree of property and independence. The ascent to better circumstances is open and they are very few who do not attempt to rise. Even if a man fails himself to escape out of the position of a wage-earner, he has hopes for his children, and is, in the mean time, profoundly convinced that the chances of life are improved almost as much by sobriety as by education. It is his reasonable ambition that makes him the ally of the social reformer and there is little fear of his trying to evade a law which he believes to be beneficial to him and his. No doubt liquor is sold on the sly in teetotal towns, just as pockets are picked, although thieving is illegal. But offenders against sobriety, in a society bent on the practice of self-restraint, will not be many. ...

The public conscience has already shut up the public-house in hundreds of New England towns. Let those who are sincerely anxious to know what results may be expected from the interference of public option with private privilege spend, as we did, a Sunday at Winsted. The order of this village, the prosperity of its operative population, the peace and purity of their lives, the independence of their characters and simplicity of their manners will be enough to convince any unprejudiced man, abstainer or not, that no greater blessing has befallen this town than the abolition of its liquor saloons.

❧ JOEL COOK ☙

J oel Cook was the Financial Editor of the Philadelphia Public Ledger who doubled as the travel writer for the paper. Frequently the newspaper would collect his previously published travel articles and re-issue them in book form. The volume from which Cook's description of Connecticut is taken, a report on life on the East Coast of the United States from Pennsylvania to Maine, is a product of that system.

Cook's work is in the mainstream of Victorian taste in both subject matter and style. Nationalistic Americans in the late nineteenth century were eager to read of the hidden glories of their native land-scape. Cook catered to an audience that demanded boosterism rather than rigorous analysis with a blend of laudatory description, colorful anecdote, and heroic myth. His unremitting emphasis is on the positive. The town of Fairfield is "tranquil." Bridgeport's "magnificent streets display splendid dwellings." New Haven "has tastefully adorned suburbs, where the hills and elevated roadways afford charming prospects." Hartford's "picturesque suburbs" are filled with "magnificent villas." Samuel Colt's employees are "very intelligent looking workingmen."

Cook's comments about Connecticut, though uncritical, do have considerable merit. He traveled through the state by railroad, and his recording of the scene that unfolded before him as he rumbled along the track captures what nineteenth-century visitors to Connecticut would have experienced. Some passages, such as his portrait of East and West Rock outside of New Haven, are quite graphic. But even the more routine descriptions of farms, factories, cities, rivers, rock outcroppings, and salt marshes attest to the variety of human and physical features that characterized this small state.

H.J.

1889   From the Grand Central Station of the Vanderbilt Lines, on forty-second Street in New York City, the New Haven Railroad carries us into New England. The line runs out of town through long tunnels, and then, skirting Central Park, turns north-east across the Harlem River, through Morrisania, Fordham, and a succession of attractive villages among the hills and rocks, until it runs along and finally crosses the pretty little Bronx River on the northern border of Bronx Park. Swiftly rolls the train along the edge of Woodlawn Cemetery, where Jay Gould has built the magnificent mausoleum for his final home. Traversing

Excerpted from Joel Cook, *An Eastern Tour of Home*, Philadelphia, David McKay, 1889.

a region of market-gardens and patches of forest, sprinkled with ... rocks and dotted over with villas, the line passes New Rochelle, where the French Huguenot refugees settled two centuries ago after Richelieu had driven them out of La Rochelle. Here in his declining years lived the noted Tom Paine upon an estate given him by the New York State Government. The most prolific crop borne in the country hereabout is rocks, and the few patient husbandmen who still remain here to battle with Nature have gathered the loose stones into piles for fences, which cross the land in all directions. This rocky development is most profuse at the village of Mamaroneck, which in the Indian tongue means "the place of rolling stones." Once in a while a serious effort is made to till this stony land. Over the mazy lines of stone fences and rocks of all kinds, a hundred yards away may be seen a man with a yoke of oxen trying to plow, but scarcely moving, for he has to go slow lest the plow strike a sunken crag and cause a catastrophe. The farther we go the greater the development of rocks, the bright foliage of the trees springing up among them making a pleasing contrast. Thus moving, about twenty-five miles from New York the train crosses Byram River, and we are in New England, which the old saying announces as stretching "from Quoddy Head to Byram River." This original Yankee-land, although the smallest section of the United States, has made the deepest impress upon the American character, and has carried the banner of enterprise and colonization throughout the entire Western country. In ideas and thought, as well as in migration, the New Englanders are usually our leaders, being the people of most advanced views in politics and religion, and usually the pioneers of radicalism. They have not enjoyed the agricultural advantages of other sections, the bleak climate, poor soil, and generous distribution of rocks and sterility making farming hard work with meagre results, so that the chief Yankee energies have been devoted to developing vast manufacturing industries, literature, commerce, and the fisheries; in short, the Yankees have had to live by their wits, and have most admirably succeeded. All the six New England States are not much larger than New York in surface, while their population is much less; but the indomitable spirit of the Pilgrims and other religious enthusiasts who were the earliest settlers implanted the untiring energy that has carried New-England ideas, methods, and population all over New York and the great West.

We have crossed the little Byram River into Connecticut, and in the intervals of rocks the train goes over inlet after inlet thrust up into the land from Long Island Sound, each having its galaxy of little rounded islets set in the entrance and its sloping shores studded with attractive villas embosomed in foliage. The glimpse along each inlet gives pretty though brief views over the distant waters of the sound, with the sun shining on the white-winged yachts beyond. Sharp is the contrast between Connecticut and New York City, so recently left behind us. With a population scarcely one-fourth the millions of souls clustering around New York harbor, yet this "Land of Steady Habits" has always made the deeper impress upon the character and policy of the country. The guiding hands and ingenious brains ruling New York business affairs are largely transplants from Connecticut and New England. De Tocqueville pointedly illustrated the subtle influence in a little speech he made after his American visit at a Fourth-of-July dinner in Paris. In his quaint broken English he said:

"Von de I vos in the gallery of the House of Representatives. I held in my hand a map of the Confederation. Dere vos von leetle yellow spot called Connect-de-coot. I found by de Constitution he was entitled to six of his boys to represent him on dat floor. But when I make the acquaintance personel with the member, I find dat more than thirty (30) of the Representatives on dat floor was born in Connect-de-coot. And den ven I vos in de gallery of the House of the Senate, I find de Constitution permit dis State to send two of his boys to represent him in dat legislature. But once there, ven I make de acquaintance personel of the Senator, I find nine of the Senator was born in Connect-de-coot.

"And now for my grand sentiment: Connect- de-coot—de leetle yellow spot dat make de clock-peddler, de schoolmaster, and de Senator; de first give you time, de second tell you what to do with him, and de third make your law and civilization."

This wonderful little State covers only four thousand seven hundred square miles, and, excepting Rhode Island and Delaware, is the smallest in the Union. It is the special land of "Yankee notions." It gave the country the original personation of "Brother Jonathan" in Governor Jonathan Trumbull, who was so useful a coadjutor to Washington. Consulting him in many emergencies, Washington was wont to remark, "Let us hear what Brother Jonathan says"—a phrase finally popularly adopted and making him the national impersonation. It has the great Puritan college of the country—Yale—ruled by the Congregationalists. It has more varied and more productive manufactures than any other people of similar means. Its abundant water-powers contribute to this, and nearly all its inhabitants are engaged in manufacturing of one kind or another. Its machinery and methods are largely the inventions or improvements of its own people, among whom three stand out prominently: Eli Whitney, of the cotton gin; Samuel Colt, of the revolver; and Charles Goodyear, of India-rubber fame. The inventive talent of the State is such that its people proportionately get more patents than those of any other, one to every eight hundred inhabitants being annually granted. Such is the diversified genius that has made Connecticut the "Wooden Nutmeg State," and De Tocqueville rightly called it the "leetle yellow spot dat make de clock-peddler," for Connecticut has almost monopolized clock-making for all the world. It leads in the production of India-rubber and elastic goods, in hardware and in myriads of ingenious "Yankee notions," and is also very near the front rank in making sewing-machines and arms and war material. Its name comes from the chief New England river—Connecticut meaning the "Long River"—flowing down from the White Mountains to the sound. Its rugged surface is diversified by long ridges of hills and deep valleys, generally running from north to south, the prolongation of mountain-ranges beyond the northern border. Through the western counties the picturesque Housatonic comes down from the Massachusetts Berkshire hills; the centre is crossed by the Connecticut Valley, a region of beautiful scenery and great fertility; while in Eastern Connecticut the Quinnebaug makes a deep valley, and, finally flowing into the Thames, seeks the sea at New London. The many hills make many streams, and wherever one is large enough to make a water-power, there clusters a nest of busy factories.

Our train glides through Greenwich, the south-western town of New England, and as we enter the Yankee-land on a high hill stands the Puritan outpost—the stately graystone Congregational church with its tall spire. The town stretches up to the wooded slopes north of the railway and away to the edge of the sound on the south. It was here that General Putnam in 1779, to get away from the British dragoons, swiftly galloped down the rude rocky stairway leading from the old church, while their bullets rattled around him. "Old Put's Hill" is there, looking much as it did in his day. The train rolls along past attractive inlets and harbors, one of the prettiest being Mianus River, with Cos Cob on its bank just beyond Greenwich. The railway winds among more rocky regions with their brilliant adornments of foliage, and soon passes picturesque Stamford, where twelve thousand people are gathered upon the hills and vales covered with the homes of New York business-men who come out to this lovely place to live. Their dwellings show good taste in architecture and embellishment, and the busy factories reflect the prevalent phase of Connecticut life. Here in the last century lived Colonel Davenport, whom the poet Whittier immortalized. He was a legislator and described as "a man of stern integrity and generous benevolence." When, in 1780, the memorable "Dark Day" came in New England, some one, fearing it was the day of judgment, proposed that the House adjourn. He opposed it, saying, "The day of judgment is either approaching or it is not; if it is, I choose to be found doing my duty. I wish, therefore, that candles may be brought." South Norwalk is another nest of busy mills, within an outer setting of wooden houses that spreads up into Norwalk beyond. The thrifty settlers hereabout originally bought a tract which extended one day's "north walk" from the sound, and hence the name. Fine oysters are gathered in its spacious bay, and the white sails of the pungies add charms to the harbor view. There are ten thousand people in these twin factory-towns, who make shoes and hats and door-knobs and locks, and when the day's labor is ended enjoy the attractive land—and water—views that are all about. On the lowlands to the eastward the noted Pequot Indian nation, once ruling this region, was finally overpowered by the colonial troops, and the Sasco Swamp, in which they were captured, now has cattle grazing and oxen plodding upon almost the only good land seen on the route. Thus we come to tranquil old Fairfield, introduced by a rubber-factory and embowered in trees. Its green-bordered streets are lined with cottages, and the church-spires rise among the groves, while along the shore it has the finest beach on Long Island Sound.

The Pequannock River is crossed a few miles farther on, with the busy city of Bridgeport on its banks. The train runs in among the enormous mills that have gathered forty thousand people here—a hive containing some of the greatest establishments in the world for making sewing-machines and firearms. Here are the huge factories of the Wheeler & Wilson and Howe Sewing-Machine Companies, Sharp's Rifle Company, and the Union Metallic Cartridge Company, with some of the greatest carriage-building shops in the country. Cutlery and corsets, carpets, organs, and soap also occupy attention. The esplanade of Seaside Park overlooks the harbor and sound beyond, and toward the north the city stretches up the slopes into Golden Hill, named from its glittering mica deposits, where magnificent streets display splendid dwellings. But the lion of Bridgeport is P.T. Barnum, who is passing his ripe old age in the stately villa of Waldemere. The veteran showman first developed the financial advantages of amusing, and possibly humbugging, the public on a great scale, and also (with Jenny Lind) started the American fashion of paying extravagant sums to opera-singers, giving her one thousand dollars for each of one hundred and fifty nights of concert-singing. He introduced Tom Thumb, who was born in Bridgeport, to an admiring world, and his "great moral shows" are familiar travelling caravans through the country. But Bridgeport is left behind, and then in quiet old Stratford, in marked contrast, it is seen that the new and active order of things has not yet wholly disturbed the old, and that neither hotel nor factory encumbers the greensward or encroaches upon its sleepy houses, where one may dream away a sweet twilight under the shade of grand trees even more ancient than the village. Beyond we cross the broad bosom of the placid Housatonic, and over patches of marshland come to Milford, with its long stretch of village green neatly enclosed, and its houses upon the bank of the silvery Wap-o-wang, back of which spread the wide streets lined by rows of overarching elms. A colony from Milford in England settled this place two hundred and fifty years ago, and, managing to crowd the Indians off the land, established the primitive church, this being the usual beginning of all New England settlements. Then, true to the American instinct, they at once proceeded to hold a convention, the result being the unanimous adoption of the following:

"Voted, That the earth is the Lord's, and the fulness thereof.

"Voted, That the earth is given to the saints."

"Voted, That we are the saints."

The descendants of these pioneer saints of Milford now make straw hats for the country. Beyond the town the railway crosses a broad expanse of salt-marshes, and the train soon halts at New Haven.

The magnificent elms of the city of New Haven, arching over the streets and the Public Green and grandly rising in stately rows, make the earliest and the deepest impression upon the visitor. In one of his most eloquent passages the late Henry Ward Beecher said the elms of New England

"...magnificent elms...arching over the streets and the Public Green...make the earliest and deepest impression..."

—*Joel Cook*

ELM ARCADE, NEW HAVEN, BY JON FILMER AFTER A.C. WARREN. WOOD ENGRAVING, N.D. (DETAIL)

are as much a part of her beauty as the columns of the Parthenon were the glory of its architecture. Sharing this feeling, one goes about the Academic City, and can readily appreciate the admiration all true New Englanders have for their favorite tree. The grand foliage-arched avenues of New Haven are unsurpassed elsewhere, so that they are the crowning glory as well as the constant care of the town. Among the finest of these avenues is the one separating the grounds of Yale College from the beautiful Public Green of the city—a magnificent Gothic aisle of rich green foliage-covered interlacing boughs. While these trees contribute so much to the beauty and notoriety of New Haven, its greatest fame comes from the possession of Yale College, one of the most extensive and comprehensive universities in the world. For almost two centuries this noble foundation has exerted a widely-diffused and advantageous influence upon the American intellectual character, and around it and its multitude of buildings of every kind now clusters New Haven town. This college began in a very small way at Saybrook, at the mouth of the Connecticut River, in 1701, and had only one student during its first year. Subsequently, for a more convenient location, it was removed to New Haven, the first commencement there being in 1718, and its first college building was then named Yale College—a name afterward adopted in the incorporation of the university, and given in honor of Elihu Yale, a native of the town, who went abroad and afterward became governor of the East India Company. He made at different times gifts of books and money amounting to about five hundred pounds sterling, his benefactions being of much greater value on account of their timeliness.

Yale is the orthodox Congregationalist college of New England, usually having over one hundred instructors in the various departments, and about eleven hundred students. Its buildings are of various ages and styles of architecture, the original ones being the plain-looking "Old Brick Row," north-west of the New Haven Public Green, behind which what was formerly an open space has become gradually covered with more modern structures, while various others, such as the Peabody

Museum, the Sheffield Scientific School, and the Divinity Halls, are located on adjacent grounds. The line of ancient college buildings in the "Old Brick Row" facing the Public Green has quite a venerable and scholarly aspect, one of the best of them, "Connecticut Hall," having been built with money raised by a lottery and from the proceeds of a French prize-ship captured in the colonial wars antedating the Revolution, when Connecticut aided King George by equipping a frigate. This row stretches broadly across the greensward, fronted by stately arching elms arranged in quadruple lines. Besides the great value of its land and buildings, Yale College has an invested fund of some one million seven hundred thousand dollars, and its annual income, including the tuition fees, is about three hundred thousand dollars. The Peabody Museum contains one of the best collections of curiosities in the country, and the Yale Library is extensive. There are scores of buildings of all kinds— from the grand academic halls down to the windowless and mysterious mausoleum that I am told entombs the "Skull-and-Bones Society"— occupying the spacious grounds of this famous college.

The Indian name for the region round about New Haven was Quinnepiack, and to this day the placid Quinnepiack River flows through a deep valley past the noted "East Rock" into the harbor. Old John Davenport was the leader and first pastor of the infant colony that settled here—an earnest preacher, revered by the Indians as "so big study man," who delivered the original sermon on founding the town from the text: "Wisdom hath builded her house; she hath hewn out her seven pillars." From this came the original scheme of government for the colony by the seven leading church members, who were known as the "seven pillars." It has since greatly grown, probably in some other things than in the quality of its piety, and, like all these Connecticut towns, is a busy hive of industry. Its many mills make agricultural machinery, corsets, scales, carriages, organs, and pianos, with a vast amount of "Yankee notions" of various kinds and miscellaneous hardware. There is also some commerce, chiefly with the West Indies and along the coast, and numerous railways fetch in the trade of the surrounding country. New Haven has tastefully adorned suburbs, where the hills and elevated roadways afford charming prospects. In the outlying regions, however, the great attractions are the two bold and striking promontories known as the East and West Rocks, which are high buttresses of trap rock lifting themselves from the plain upon which New Haven is chiefly built, one on each side of the town, in a magnificent array of opposition, and each rising over four hundred feet. Some of the inhabitants think these grim precipices in remote ages may have sentinelled the outflow of the Connecticut River between their broad and solid bases to the sound. Each of these tremendous cliffs is the termination of a long ridge or mountain-range that comes down from the far North. The Green Mountain outcropping, stretching southward from Vermont, is represented in the West Rock, while the East Rock terminates what is known as the Mount Tom range, through which the Connecticut River breaks a passage up in Massachusetts, and part of which rises a thousand feet in the "Blue Hills of Southington," making the most elevated lands in the State of Connecticut. The summits of these two great rocks, thus projected out toward Long Island Sound, afford grand views. In a cave upon the West Rock the three regicides, Goffe, Whalley, and Dixwell, were in hiding, and the three avenues leading to this rock from the city are named after them. Dixwell's bones repose upon the Public Green at the back of the "Centre Church," which stands in the row of three churches occupying the middle of the green, which was the common graveyard of colonial New Haven. The approach to the East Rock, going out Orange Street, is grand. The rock is elevated high above the marshy valley of Mill River winding about its base, and reared upon the topmost crag is a noble monument erected by New Haven in memory of the soldiers who fell in the Civil War—a magnificent shaft overlooking the town and valley that is seen from afar. The whole surface of the East Rock is reserved as a public park. Upon the face of the cliff the perpendicular strata of reddish-

brown trap stand bolt upright. There are well-laid roads of easy gradi-
ent gradually rising through the bordering ravines and amid the forest
until the top is reached, where from this elevated outpost there is a charming view. Far over the flat plain to the southward spreads the town, with
its little harbor stretching out into the sound, and beyond, across the
silvery waters, there can be seen the distant hazy shores of Long
Island, twenty-five miles away. The numerous wooden houses nestle
among the trees, and the two little crooked rivers coming out of the deep
valleys on either side of the great rock wind onward to mingle their waters
in the harbor. Smoke ascends from the numerous factory-chimneys down
by the water-side, while all around the country is dotted with flourishing
villages. This is the noble outlook over the "City of Elms" and its pleasant surroundings as seen from this grand outpost rising high above the
plain upon which the Academic City is built.

Almost under the shadow of the towering East Rock is laid the railway connecting New Haven with Hartford, and thence it passes northward along the valley of Quinnepiack River over flat meadow-land bordered by blue hills. Brick-making seems to be the chief industry on these
meadows, and they are prolific grass-growers, judging by the hundreds
of little haystacks dotted over them. Soon, however, sterility is devel
oped, for vast sand-deposits overlie the soil, and farming here must be
a discouraging occupation. These moors, with their sands and sloughs
and scrub timber, demonstrate the plight of the average Connecticut
settler, for, being unable to wrest a living out of the land, he either has
to go to making "Yankee notions" or emigrate or starve. Wallingford is
passed, its church-towers crowning the hill to the eastward of the railway and watching over a population largely made up of German-silver
and plated-ware manufacturers. When this town was founded John
Davenport was invited to come out from New Haven and conduct the
religious services. He came and preached the initial sermon from a text
regarded as appropriate to the locality: "My beloved hath a vineyard on

a fruitful hill." Beyond, and nestling under the shadow of the "Blue Hills of Southington," is Meriden. These hills rise high above its western and northern borders in the West Park and Mount Lamentation. Here is another active hive of factories fringed around with the neat wooden dwellings of their operatives, while the villas of their owners are scattered about in pleasant places upon the steep declivities of the adjacent hills. These people are industrious workers in iron and steel, in bronze and brass, in making tin, Britannia, and electro-plated silverware. The chief establishment of the place is the well-known Meriden Britannia Company, its enormous mills being spread for a long distance along the railway and making the greatest manufactory of its kind in the world, sending out over five million dollars' worth of its wares in a year.

Meriden and Berlin, a short distance northward, are the headquarters of the peripatetic Connecticut tin-peddler, who starts out laden with all kinds of tin pans and pots and other bright and useful utensils to wander over the country and charm the rural housewife with his bargains. Berlin began the first American manufacture of tinware in the last century. While it bears an ambitious German name, it was started by a colony of shrewd Yankees. These New England villages—and there are hundreds like them—all seem to be cast in the same mould and to have similar characteristics. There are in each the beautiful central public green shaded by rows of stately elms; the tall-spired churches; the village graveyard, usually sloping down a hillside, with the lines of white gravestones supplemented in the modern interments by more elaborate monuments; the attractive wooden houses nestling amid foliage and surrounded by gardens and flower-beds, the homes of the people; and the big factories that give them employment. Some of these villages, being larger than others, may show a greater development in various ways, but, excepting in size, all are substantially alike. The ox-team slowly plods along the road, and the scanty crop in the field shows how the sand and stones have choked the efforts of the husbandman. And, thus gliding along past village and mill, there soon comes into view the distant gilded dome of the Connecticut State Capitol, and finally the broad fronts of the buildings of Trinity College surmounting Rocky Hill. The train runs among a labyrinth of factories down upon the edge of the little Park River, and soon halts at the station, under the shadow of the Capitol, in the centre of the city of Hartford, on the Connecticut River.

The noted Adriaen Block, the Dutch navigator, built at the Battery in New York in 1614 the first ship ever constructed in New York harbor. The four little huts he put up to house his crew and builders were among the first structures of the early colony. His blunt-pointed Knickerbocker yacht of sixteen tons he named the "Onrest," and in her started on a voyage of discovery through Hellgate into Long Island Sound. To him belongs the honor of discovering on this important voyage the principal river of New England, and after his explorations he rested on the land that still bears his name—Block Island. The sources of the Connecticut River are in the highlands bordering Canada at an elevation of more than sixteen hundred feet above the sea, and it flows southwest over four hundred miles to Long Island Sound. The Indians called it "Quoncktakat," or the "Long River," and hence the name and that of the "Nutmeg State" wherein it finds its mouth. The river has always been noted for beautiful scenery, and has many cataracts, among them South Hadley in Massachusetts and Enfield in Connecticut, furnishing abundant water-power to the mills lining the banks. It flows into the sound thirty-three miles east of New Haven, at Saybrook. ...

... The lower Connecticut flows through a prolific agricultural region, with lands enriched by copious dressings of fish-manures got from the river. It passes picturesque shores and sundry farming-villages below Middletown, amid scenes that in a diminished sort of way are reminders of the hills along the Hudson. Another nest of active mills is at Middletown, making plated wares, pumps, and webbing, sewing-machines and tapes. Its shaded streets lead up the hill-slopes here enclosing the river that have within their recesses valuable quarries of Portland stone. The court-house is a quaint little miniature of the Parthenon. The Wesleyan Methodist College is located here, Memorial and Judd Halls being grand buildings. North of Middletown, green, level, and exceedingly fertile meadows adjoin the river, their great yield being the noted onion crops of Wethersfield. This was the earliest Connecticut settlement, and its onions permeate the whole country. It is historic, too, for here convened the first Connecticut legislature to declare war against the Pequots in 1636, while one of the old mansions of the town is pointed out as the place where Washington and the French officers prepared the plans which ended the Revolution by the great victory at Yorktown.

We have ascended the Connecticut River to the State Capital, the noted city which repeats in this newer land the name in the mother-country of the ancient Saxon village at the "Ford of Harts," whence some of its first settlers came. It was the brave and pious Thomas Hooker who led his flock from the sea-coast through the wilderness to Hartford to establish an English settlement at the Indian post of Suckiang, where the Dutch had previously built a fort and trading-station at the bend of the river. That quaint historian of early New England, Cotton Mather, afterward described Hooker as "the renowned minister of Hartford and pillar of Connecticut, and the light of the Western churches." This lovely and most substantial city well deserves its favorite title of "The Queen." Its centre is a beautiful park, in front of which the narrow and winding stream known as Park River flows down to the Connecticut. From the railway-station a light bridge leads over this little river to the triumphal brownstone arch with surmounting conical towers which is the tasteful entrance to the park. This arch honors the men sent out from the city who served and fell during the Civil War. A grand highway then continues up the hill to the Capitol building, the finest structure in New England, an imposing

Gothic edifice of white marble three hundred feet long, all its fronts being elaborately ornamented with statuary and artistic decoration, while the high surmounting gilded dome rises two hundred and fifty feet. The interior is well lighted, and seems to be thoroughly adapted to the purposes of the State Government and the halls of the legislature of the "Nutmeg State." Rugged and famous old General Israel Putnam, the idol of this land of steady habits, has his statue in the Capitol grounds; he died here in 1790. "The Putnam Phalanx" is the crack military company of Hartford, a body dressing in an antique Continental uniform and having a membership of about one hundred and twenty-five of the wealthiest townsmen. Within the Capitol is the bronze statue of Nathan Hale of Connecticut, whom the British during the Revolution executed as a spy. It is one of the most striking masterpieces of sculpture. The almost living figure seems animated with the full vigor of earnest youth, and with outstretched hands actually appears to speak his memorable words: "I only regret that I have but one life to lose for my country." The battered and weather-worn gravestone that originally covered Putnam's grave is also kept as a precious relic, and alongside of it are cases containing the battered battle-flags of the Connecticut regiments. Within the gorgeous Assembly Chamber, which is the gem of this magnificent building, the law-makers, it is hoped, now enact milder legislation than the rigorous "Connecticut blue laws" of the olden time, when the iron rule of the stern Puritan pastors, then governing the colony, created a Draconian code inflicting death-penalties for the crimes of idolatry, unchastity, blasphemy, witchcraft, murder, man-stealing, smiting parents, and some others, while savage laws also punished Sabbath-breaking and the use of tobacco.

Much of Hartford clusters around the "Charter Oak," although that famous tree is now only a memory revered by the townspeople. Thirty-two years ago it was blown down in a storm, and its remains were made into many precious relics. Our old friend "Mark Twain," who lives in

Hartford, and therefore knows much of the matter, says he has seen all conceivable articles made out of this precious timber, there being, among others, "a walking-stick, dog-collar, needle-case, three-legged stool, boot-jack, dinner-table, ten-pin alley, toothpick, and enough Charter Oak to build a plank road from Hartford to Great Salt Lake City." This ancient tree concealed the original royal character of the colony when, in 1687, the tyrannical governor Andros demanded its surrender. While the subject was being discussed in the legislature the lights were put out, and in the darkness a bold colonist seized it, and, running out, hid the precious document in the hollow of the oak. A marble slab now marks the place on "Charter Oak Hill" where the tree stood alongside "Charter Oak Place," and "Charter Oak Avenue" leads up to it. The fine statue surmounting the Capitol dome and representing the female genius of Connecticut, which overlooks the city with outstretched hand, is crowning the municipality with a wreath of Charter Oak leaves. The oak leaf is repeated in many ways in the gorgeous decoration within and upon the Capitol building, and also upon many structures throughout the city. The name of "Charter Oak" is given to a bank, a life-insurance company, and many other institutions of the solid community which is blessed with this honored memory.

Hartford, in proportion to its population, is the wealthiest American city. It is financially great, particularly in insurance, there being no less than twenty-one fire and life companies, some of them of great strength and doing business in all parts of the world. Its Charter Oak Insurance Company dwells in a granite palace on Main Street, and some others, such as the Hartford, the Aetna, the Connecticut Mutual, and the Phoenix, also have fine buildings. These companies have a widespread business, and some of them enormous capitals and assets. The city also has many strong banks, and is renowned for its numerous charitable institutions, its extensive book-publishing houses, and its educational foundations, the most noted being Trinity College. From the elevated position of this college there is a grand view across the intervening valley to the hills of Farmington and westward to Talcott Mountain. The vast wealth of the Hartford people has enabled them to enrich its picturesque suburbs, so that an extensive district around it is covered with magnificent villas, making a semi-rural residential section that is unsurpassed by any other New England city. Arching elms, as everywhere else, embower here the lawn-bordered avenues that stretch for long distances, and in many localities the superb hedges impart quite an English air. Some of the splendid suburban homes of the "Queen City" are perfect gems of artistic construction and attractive decoration, the evidences of the wealth of the people being shown on all sides. There is also a devotion to art, the galleries of the Wadsworth Atheneum having a fine collection. Among the relics kept here are General Putnam's sword and the old Indian King Philip's club.

But the citizen whom Hartford seems to hold in highest esteem is the late Colonel Samuel Colt, who invented the revolving pistol. He was a native of Hartford, and his remains rest under a noble monument in Cedar Hill Cemetery. A beautiful little brownstone Gothic chapel, the "Church of the Good Shepherd," has been built in his memory. Colt when a boy ran away from home and went to sea, and is said to have there conceived the idea of his great invention. During several years he sought with indifferent success to establish an arms manufactory. He did not prosper until 1852, when he started a factory in Hartford, and with the great demand for small-arms then stimulated by the opening of the California gold-mines and the exploration of the Western Plains, and afterward vastly expanded by the necessities created by the Civil War, his factory grew into an enormous business. "The Colt Arms Company," which was for many years managed by General Franklin, is the chief industrial establishment of Hartford, having very large buildings adjacent to the Connecticut River that are filled with the latest appliances and machinery for making the most approved arms of all kinds. These mills, however, thrive only on war, and it may gratify our Peace Society to know that they are now running very light, though still making a goodly number to supply a demand for pistols and rifles that is constant. They employ a small army of very intelligent-looking workmen, who appear to be in advance of the average in intellectuality. Throughout these vast works there is everywhere seen a reminder of the great Hartford inventor in the representation of his family coat-of-arms, the heraldic "colt rampant," which is stamped upon all the arms and impressed and reproduced upon all the adornments of this greatest Hartford establishment.

A short distance north of Hartford is the imaginary line that marks the Massachusetts southern boundary. We follow up the Connecticut Valley, which is here a broad and comparatively level region of good land, with the placid river flowing through it. We have temporarily left the region of sand and stones so well developed in the "Nutmeg State," and come into the rich meadows of Mattaneag, a fertile intervale, where the fences are built of wood, as stones seem scarce. Its entrepot is Windsor, an agricultural colony started by John Worham, who, the local historian says, was the first New England pastor who used notes in preaching. Whether he defied the "blue laws" by using tobacco we are not told, but his colony is to-day a great tobacco-growing section, through which the Farmington River flows down from the western hills. The Enfield Rapids of the Connecticut are here, and a canal formerly used to take the river-craft around the obstruction now gives ample water-power to many paper and other mills that make the town of Windsor Locks. The river flows swiftly over its pebbly bed, being dammed above to divert some of the water into the canal. The Hazardville Powder-Works are not far away, the greatest gunpowder-factory in America, and Thompsonville is adjacent, a maker of carpets to a prodigious extent. Then we cross the boundary into the "Old Bay State," the chief New England commonwealth, also largely a nest of factories, and the leading State of the Union in the manufacture of cotton and woollen goods, boots and shoes, leather and paper.

❧ AGNES WATSON ☙

I n the autumn of 1889, Agnes Watson, the Scottish niece of a Glastonbury tobacco farmer, Henry Affleck, began a holiday tour of America by visiting her uncle in Glastonbury. With her were her husband, Adam Watson, who appears to have been in the textile trade, and Maggie, one of their children. At that time, the town of Glastonbury was a small farming community of widely scattered houses. "We at home would not call it a town," she wrote in one of her many letters home. "A settlement would be the correct name for it."

Arriving in New York, the Watsons immediately inquired about transportation to Glastonbury, "which seemed to be a place that no one knew anything about." They began their trip on one of New York's elevated railways, which took them to 42nd street and a horse railway, which in turn bought them to Grand Central station and a steam train to New Haven, where they changed to the Air Line to Middletown and then changed again for Rocky Hill, where a mail gig took them on the ferry and a six mile ride through "back woods" to Glastonbury, where they were warmly welcomed by their relatives.

Agnes Watson's letters give a view of small-town life in Connecticut at the end of the late nineteenth century. She was determined to enjoy what she found in America, and she did: a congregation all fanning themselves during a sermon; grapes hanging within reach from above a veranda; mosquitoes so unbelievably big that she sent specimens home in a letter; "villas" in Middletown that "would put to shame all that we have in the old country" but that "cost little money, being built of wood with brick foundations"; the Cheney silk mills in Manchester, where "they have railways of their own running to and from the usual lines" and where, as each Cheney son marries, "a mansion is built for him, and there he remains"; in Hartford she sees what she takes to be "the State chair of the Governor of the United States."

B. McK.

171

Glastonbury, Conn., 30th August 1889.

1889

My dear little Nan,

How pleased you will be to have a letter from mother! I hope it finds you well, and the boys very good to you.

On Wednesday morning the immense steamship "City of Paris" steamed past us into the harbour. She did the voyage in five days. We stepped from off our ship at 8 A.M. on Wednesday. What a vast and magnificent city New York is! What a go-ahead people the Americans are! If they would only stop now, and fill in the details, as it were, they would do themselves credit. For instance, the meanest lane in Scotland is a king of roads when compared to any one of theirs. After having had our boxes examined, and no fault being found, we had them fixed up again (poor father had an awful time of it, no help being given).

We posted our letters, and after infinite labour we gathered information about Glastonbury, which seemed to be a place that no one knew anything about. According to directions given we walked to a line of steam cars, where we were told to ride to 42nd Street. We went up three very high stairs to reach the cars. They run on rails laid upon iron pillars as high as the top of the houses. The carriages and carts do their work on the street below. At 42nd Street we got into a horse-car, and were taken to the "Great Central Station," to which place our luggage had been sent. We were just in time to get a train to Newhaven. The railway cars are a treat. You go in at one end, and can walk right through. They are fitted up like drawing-rooms, and contain smoking and luncheon rooms. From Newhaven we had to find our way to the air line for Middletown. That journey occupied two hours. Arrived there, we found we had to wait till 4:30 for a train to Rockiehill. We consoled ourselves by hiring a carriage and driving round Middletown, a good-sized town, whose handsome villas would put to shame all we have in the old country. They cost little money, being built of wood with brick foundations.

Excerpted from Agnes Watson, *Our Trip to America: Being Diary and Letters written during a Holiday Tour in the Autumn of 1889*, Edinburgh, Oliver and Boyd, 1890.

On reaching Rockiehill we were handed over to the mail-gig. The driver chanced to be a right good fellow, and, joy of joys, he knew Henry Affleck, who, he said, was one of the good sort. We then got into the mail-gig, the boxes being strapped on behind. Fixed thus we drove a little way, then crossed a ferry. The road again for six miles seemed to us to cut through the back-woods. It was now 8 o'clock. In all we had done 180 miles. Our feelings by this time were down to zero. It seemed so strange that no one was meeting us. Uncle's house was reached at last; all was still and quiet. Our driver went in first to break the news of our arrival to uncle, and I followed. He was resting on a couch, and was not startled. He saved himself by beginning to abuse us for not telling him the name of the ship by which we were coming. I directed my last letter to Mrs. Hardin, who was from home, and her husband did not open it. He did not think it was from us, having the Carnwath post-mark on it. He was quite sorry, as he meant to meet us at New York, and bring us here by the river. Well, all here have given us a cordial welcome. Dear old uncle is glad; he cannot sit still, always going round to have us made comfortable.

Glastonbury is a town with post-office, manufactories, such as soap-works, a tannery, a creamery, and shirt and collar factories. The buildings are far apart, with plenty of ground round them. Uncle lives in a fine house of many rooms and three flats, with a verandah round the sitting-room flat. I am sitting there now, and what do you think is growing over me? Only vines, from which endless bunches of purple grapes are hanging. The gardener says, "Go pick 'em, they ain't no use to us." I ate one large bunch this morning. I thought to myself it was just what would have been divided among seven at home. Maggie and I have eaten half-a-dozen pears each besides; verily we shall be ill. I wish I had my dear children to share them with me. Uncle owns a fine place here. Tobacco is grown upon it. Apple trees are abundant everywhere; the melons and cucumbers grow outside, while tomatoes are as common as our currant bushes. Lovely flowers and fine shrubs grow around us; outside and inside of the house seems a paradise to Maggie and me. Uncle has a pleasant old lady for a housekeeper, who desires me to give you all her best respects. ... Uncle has two carriages and one very fine horse. Sam also has two carriages and two horses. All horses in this country have long tails. People pride themselves on the length of their horses' tails and manes.

Uncle and father have been to the races to-day. Father was delighted; he says he could not look at any of our races again. He saw a horse that challenged the world as a trotter. He went off with his team ... and covered one mile in the fast time of 2 minutes 9¼ seconds. ... The worst of it is, that most carriages hold only two people. The wheels put me in mind of bicycle wheels.

I wish Eddie to know that the potato crop in America is this year an utter failure, owing to the heavy rains. They have just ploughed what was [left] of them into the ground. Uncle says they will have to be imported, and that should raise their price in the old country. I wish Eddie could see the handsome bullocks that do the carting here; a couple are passing by now, drawing a great cart of hay.

We hope to have your letter tomorrow with news of home. The mosquitoes are biting me like fun. They do not trouble sister; she must not be so sweet. It is now evening; we have been wandering up and down. I have seen no birds here; but now there is much music in the air. ...

Now, my dear little girl, all our loves to you, Adam, Eddie, and Finlay. I will write to "Lawyer Fin" next time. Remember me to everybody. Love and a kiss to you, my dear, from
Your loving Mother.

Glastonbury, Conn., 30th August 1889.
My dear Finlay,
...Yesterday we drove round and about Glastonbury. We at home would not call it a town, a settlement would be the correct name for it. All around it are beautiful houses, and uncle's is one of the finest, while his grounds are beautifully kept. We then went to see the peach orchards

The Connecticut Historical Society, Hartford.

"...the wheels put me in mind of bicycle wheels."

—*Agnes Watson*

START OF 2ND HEAT $10,000 TROT, HARTFORD BY FRANK G. WARNER. PHOTOGRAPH, AUGUST 28, 1889 (DETAIL)

—acres and acres growing—the trees loaded with their delicious fruit. As Libbie said, "Don't you wish your children were here?" Peaches above our heads, peaches below our feet, treading them down like "chuckie" stones. Many branches of trees were altogether on the ground, borne down by the weight of their fruit. Cousin Libbie lives just up the road, which you must understand is one long avenue of trees—fine old elms, hickory, and walnut. This avenue is lighted at night with oil-lamps, swung across the road from the branches of the trees; they have a very fine effect.

We will have them tried on our own avenue one of these days.

We spent Saturday with Libbie. She also lives in a nice house, and has plenty. We have not seen Raymond's ponies yet. We saw the pretty carriage in which they are to run as a pair. It seems the ponies are in a field one mile from here. Raymond has been travelling with his mamma in Canada all summer, and the ponies will not be in proper trim for a few days. We had a splendid dinner at Libbie's, and then walked to see the "Creamery"—a place for Eddie to see. All the better-class people here keep cows; the cream is gathered and sold to this creamery. They turn out 190 lbs. of butter three times a week. It is all salted, as the people here don't use sweet butter, because it would not keep. The heat is great to-day—90° outside and 75° indoors—the houses being kept very cool. ...

This morning (Sunday) we are again at Libbie's to go to church. What a beautiful church is here, with a fine organ and choir! The minister has £350 a year for stipend, with a fine manse. He got a present of a horse and buggy from his congregation. He has just left them, and sold the latter off. I guess Mr Thomson might make more here than at Liberton. We had a very poor sermon from a professor of Greek, but we had plenty to see and hear. The ladies here dress well, in the height of fashion, got from the town of Hartford, six miles distant. They mostly wear white, or the palest shades of colour. Their hats are in nowise behind, and each one carries a fan to church, and waves it continually even there; so to a stranger it has a peculiar effect. We dined and supped at Libbie's, and so passed our second Sunday from home. The mosquitoes bite me and Sam, (who is stout) awfully. They do not trouble Maggie. I send you home some dead bodies. ... The atmosphere feels lighter, and I breathe much easier in the New World. ...

Your Loving Mother.

P.S.-Papa says I am to tell you that he is walking about with only his shirt and trousers on.

Glastonbury, Conn.,2nd September 1889.
Dear Little Nest,

 ...All the little girls here dress in white or coloured muslin. They have large Leghorn hats, with lovely feathers and ribbons. They are little pale things, however, and have not got your rosy cheeks and sunny hair. Raymond is a very good boy, and very kind to Maggie and me. He is now taller and stronger, and quite a manly little fellow. Sister will have Libbie show her how to make candies. She could see how to make many beautiful cakes, but, alas! our ovens at home would not bake them. They only use American stoves here. Three little bits of wood will bake three tarts and boil the kettle for tea. There is no coal used but in winter time. ...
Your Loving Mother.

Glastonbury, Conn., 4th September 1889.
My Dear Adam,

 ...We had a great day yesterday. In the early morning we went by stagecoach to Hartford, which is now a large city. When our friends lived there it was quite a small place. It now has its banks and insurance offices, its colleges and seminaries, its orphanages, its institutions for the blind, the deaf, and the dumb. All those buildings are resplendent in architectural beauty. There is what is called the "Capitol," a vast building in which is kept the charter of American freedom, and there the law-courts are held. The Capitol is built entirely of white marble, its many pillars of Aberdeen granite, its floors of mosaic tile. Didn't I enjoy walking through its "Marble Halls!" On its summit is an immense gilded dome, surmounted by the figure of Liberty in bronze. We were partly hoisted and partly climbed to the summit— 240 feet; think of mother nothing daunted, and would not be behind. I also sat in the State chair of the Governor of the United States, a chair which cost £100 to carve out of an old oak, in which had been hidden the charter during the last war. Much ground around this building is beautifully laid out; there is also the soldiers' and sailors' monument; but, as I have bought some of the views, I shall spare you a further description.

From the Capitol, Libbie took us to a fine hotel, where we dined. We had a splendid dinner, with a choice of many dainties, but Maggie and I dined on "Blue Fish" (like our mackerel), chocolate cream, and pumpkin pie (most delicious; thought of Nancy's fairy tale), and iced water. We were waited upon by black servants—mostly coloured men and women are employed for labour. Machinery suspended from the ceiling kept sets of fanners, (such as I have seen on a windmill), in continuous motion, and these made the air delightfully cool. Afterwards, Libbie engaged a carriage and pair, and we drove to Spring-Grove Cemetery, where George Affleck lies buried; then to Zion Hill, where Uncle Henry has a monument erected to the memory of James and Jane Hunter (your great-grand-parents), ...

After saying "Good-bye" to the graves of those to whom I never hoped to be so near, we drove to Cedar Hill Cemetery. The monuments that are here erected to the dead surpass in elegance and beauty anything you can imagine. I would not now like to show to an American the finest one in our Dean Cemetery. ... At last we returned to our stage-coach, a ramshackle affair; and as for roads, the very meanest of our country lanes in Scotland is as good as the finest road in Hartford. Driving six miles from it to Glastonbury, the roads are like a ploughed field—not earth, which we are longing to see, but dust which rises up in dense clouds around us, going down our throats so that we can scarcely speak. At length we reached Libbie's, where we had tea. Sam had gone to New York yesterday on business. He is town-clerk, etc., here, and is very highly respected. Uncle's man is taking in his second crop of hay. ...
Your loving Mother.

Glastonbury, Conn., 6th September 1889.
My dear Edmonstone,
... To-day has seen us at Manchester inspecting the silk manufactories of the Cheney Brothers. We were introduced to one of the Messrs

Cheney, and shown over the mills by himself. He is fond of Scotch workmen, and has many of them holding responsible positions in his mills.
... The grounds around the works are beautiful, all greensward and trees.
They manufacture silk, velvet, and plush of all kinds for curtains and
covering furniture. What different styles for Adam to see. Mr Cheney
told us that when he was a boy the mill was so small that the machinery was driven by an engine of 6 horse power, and now there is an engine
of 600 horse power. They have railways of their own running to and from
the usual lines. ...

On Friday morning we were astir by 5 o'clock, had breakfast, then
Sam drove us to Hartford, which we reached at 8:30, arrived at
Bridgeport by 10:35, and found Mr Montignani awaiting us. How glad
we were to meet again! I think one is apt to make good friends on board
ship. We walked to his studio a short distance off. After waiting a while
his carriage came round, and we drove through the park and by the race-
course. The park extends some miles with broad carriage-ways winding through under the trees. Bridgeport is a fine town-a miniature Hartford-
but it has the advantage of being a fashionable watering-place with fine
hotels, where the general charge is 6 dollars a day. We drove past the
abode of the notorious Barnum, once Tom Thumb's keeper, and still
owner of the largest circus and troupe of wild beasts in the world. He
lives in a ducal mansion, and has his grounds laid out, father says, like
Hampton Court. They have a wonderful way of removing houses here.
They begin to pick away the foundation of brick; introducing supporters
after this, they put in rollers, and so hurl the house right along. We have
seen several under the process of removal.

We returned to Mr Montignani's and dined there. His wife is very
pleasant and very good looking. He has one son and daughter. In the
afternoon we drove to Rock Hotel on the seaside. We there rested, sitting on the piazza sipping iced lemonade through two straw quills. Before
us in the water were divers ladies and gentlemen disporting themselves,
much to your father's enjoyment. We then returned to tea, and spent

what we would call a musical evening. We thoroughly enjoyed it, because it was exactly like our own home life. Vinnie Montignani plays on the violin, and his sister, who is younger, accompanies him on the piano. He is but a learner like Finlay, so for once I felt near home.

Saturday Morning.—We said "Good-bye" to our kind friends, and started for the studio, where we had our pictures taken. These friends have been very good to us indeed. Then we made for the station and got on our way to Hartford. ...

...Yesterday forenoon father drove out with Cousin Jenny in one of her carriages. She has two with hoods, four wheels, seated for two people. One is done up in blue, the newer one in green like ours. Then she has an open carriage seated for four or five, and lastly, what would please you best, a handsome sleigh. She has a very nice place here, and is very well off. Glendale lies down in a valley among the hills. A staid and solemn river wends its way along, named the Housatonic River. From it the great Housatonic line of railway takes its name, because the cars follow its windings. When doing so, the curves of the line are so sharp that people seated in the train see the engine rounding them, and the swaying of the cars makes me think I am at sea. In the afternoon we enjoyed a drive with Jenny. The roads here are firm and good, and the land of a stony nature. Our road wound through amongst the hills. They are not like our hills, being covered to the top with pine trees. At their base grows thick bushwood, never penetrated by the foot of man. The way was one long avenue; if the folks at home had it, they would know what to do with it, and would turn it to good account. ...

Wednesday.—Father and Libbie have been paying a visit to what was once Uncle James' paper-mill. I did not go, as I wished to write this. We will set out for a drive this afternoon. We mean to leave here to-morrow for North Adams, where we will see Uncle David's widow and his family. Libbie and Jenny go with us to make a nice time of it. I shall write to Finlay next time, but I may as well tell you that we mean to leave this State on Friday morning *en route* for

Middletown, Ohio. We will do Niagara on our way. Fancy mother, old lady! Now, my dears, it is time to give our love to one and all at home. How I would like to peep in upon you! Good-bye all, with much love, and with much more than I can say. ...

Your Loving Mother.

TWENTIETH CENTURY CONNECTICUT

Two selections from the early part of the twentieth century conclude this brief volume. Both pay more attention to the darker aspects of the economic transformations accompanying industrialization than do the nineteenth-century selections that precede them.

The first brief selection, by Clifton Johnson, is included because it takes notice of the difficulties rural areas of the state could experience in finding a place in the new market economy. Saybrook owed its prominence more to its strategic position at the mouth of the Connecticut River than to the agricultural potential of its lands. Though the town center possessed the traditional green, church, and stately elms that had become the hallmarks of New England communities, and though it continued to attract wealthy residents who valued its shoreline situation, as an economic enterprise the town was clearly in decline. Clifton Johnson's portrait of two elderly siblings barely able to make ends meet from the family farm points to the difficulties experienced by those excluded from the new economic opportunities springing up in the urban areas.

Jonathan Daniels's observations about the state on the eve of World War II bring us to the age of full industrialization. The gap previously so obvious between the experiences of past visitors and a modern reader narrows. Daniels describes a world we find familiar, a world dominated by the automobile and an adult work force composed of both men and women fully integrated into the marketplace.

However, Daniels also draws our attention to ways in which the present differs from the recent past. Writing at the conclusion of the Great Depression, he underscores the degree to which what he calls the economic "pinch" generated ethnic hatred and discrimination against minorities. At the same time he celebrates the capacity of new heavy industries, particularly the aircraft industry, to expand employment and relieve economic distress.

In 1940 Daniels expressed skepticism about the adequacy of the state's resources and the ability of its Yankee leadership to deal effectively with all its problems and by implication to set a national example. While that skepticism may still seem appropriate, one thing is certain. Though the state's "Yankee" leadership is no longer distinctively British or Protestant, it continues to wrestle innovatively with difficulties that transcend the boundaries of Connecticut. It also continues to come up with solutions worthy of respectful scrutiny by those beyond its borders.

⎈∘ CLIFTON JOHNSON ∘⎈

C lifton Johnson was born in Hadley, Massachusetts, in 1865. Hadley remained his home, and he died there in 1940. By the time of his death, at age seventy-five, he had written, edited, or illustrated about a book a year through most of his working life, some fifty or more books all told, most of them recounting his travels and observations in the British Isles, France, and the United States. The account of Saybrook, below, is from his New England and its Neighbors, *1902.*

The Saybrook that Johnson visited, before the advent of commuters and summer residents in their motor cars, was "the dwelling-place of a country aristocracy," a village "neither agricultural nor suburban," where the ubiquitous bicycle could still be referred to as "this thoroughly modern contrivance." Old families in large houses lived near the cen-

ter; a little further out, the less well-off; and beyond that the country-side. Neither the comfortable nor the less well-off seemed to Johnson to share the sense of bustle and enterprise traditionally attributed to the citizens of Connecticut.

B. McN.

1902

My acquaintance with Saybrook began rather unpropitiously at its one hotel. This was a shapeless yellow structure, evidently an old residence somewhat remodelled and enlarged. Its busiest portion was the bar-room adorned with a heavy cherry counter and imposing array of bottles on the shelves behind. When I entered the adjoining office, several men were in the bar-room running over their vocabularies of swear words in a high-voiced dispute; and in the office itself sat two young fellows drowsing in drunken stupor. The whole place was permeated with the odors of liquor and with tobacco fumes, both recent and of unknown antiquity.

But if the aspect of local life as seen at the hotel was depressing, the village, on the evening I arrived, was to my eyes quite entrancing. In the May twilight I walked from end to end of the long chief street. The birds were singing, and from the seaward marshes came the piping of the frogs and the purring monotones of the toads. Lines of great elms and sugar maples shadowed the walks, and the latter had blossomed so that every little twig had its tassels of delicate yellow-green, and a gentle fragrance filled the air. Among other trees, a trifle retired, were many pleasant homes of the plain but handsome and substantial type in vogue about a century ago. In short, the place furnished an admirable example of the old New England country town, and imparted a delightful sense of repose and comfort.

The most incongruous feature of the village was an abnormal, modern schoolhouse that in its decorative trickery matched nothing else on

---

Excerpted from Clifton Johnson, *New England and its Neighbors*, New York, Macmillan Company, 1902.

the street. From this it was a relief to turn to the white, square-towered old church neighboring, which gave itself no airs and cut no capers with architectural frills and fixings. On its front was a bronze plate informing the reader that here was

THE FIRST CHURCH OF CHRIST
IN SAYBROOK
ORGANIZED
IN "THE GREAT HALL" OF THE FORT
IN THE SUMMER OF 1646

Thus it was one of the earliest founded churches in the commonwealth.

An odd thing about the town, and one that rather offset its sentiment of antiquity, was the omnipresence of bicycles. Everybody—old and young, male and female—rode this thoroughly modern contrivance. Pedestrianism had apparently gone out of fashion, and I got the idea that the children learned to ride a wheel before they began to walk.

Another odd thing was that the village looked neither agricultural nor suburban. It is in truth the dwelling-place of a country aristocracy possessed of a good deal of wealth, and labor is not very strenuous. The people are content if they have sufficient capital safely invested to return them a comfortable living and save them the necessity for undue exertion. Yet, to quote a native, "They are nothing like as rich as they were fifty years ago."

Much money has been lost in one way and another. The decrease, however, is more due to removals and to the division of large individual properties among several heirs. But, whatever the ups and downs of fortune, the town apparently changes slowly, and the inhabitants cling to the customs of their forefathers. One evidence of this was the retention of miles and miles of unnecessary fences about the dwellings, some of them of close boards, suggestive of monastic seclusiveness.

The oldest house in the town that still presents in the main its original aspect dates back to 1665. It is painted a dingy yellow, and has a high front, from which the rear roof takes a long slant downward, until the eaves are within easy reach, and you have to stoop to go in at the back door. The windows have the tiny panes of the time when the dwelling was erected. The rooms all have warped floors, and low ceilings crossed by great beams; and the heavy vertical timbers assert themselves in the corners. The upper story has only two apartments finished. As was usual in houses of this kind, the rest was left simply garret space bare to the rafters. In the heart of the structure is an enormous chimney that on the ground floor takes up the space of a small room. There are fireplaces on three sides, but their days of service are past, though they never have been closed except with fireboards.

At the rear of the house, under an apple tree, were two vinegar barrels, each of which had an inverted bottle stuck in the bung-hole. The contents of the barrels, in their cider state, had been allowed to freeze and then were drained off. A highly concentrated beverage was in this manner obtained, much esteemed by the well-seasoned cider-lover. I was offered a chance to make the acquaintance of the liquor, yet not without warning that, as it was almost pure alcohol, there was some danger of overdoing the matter.

To the north of the town one does not have to follow the highways far to encounter country that, with all the years passed since the settlement of the region, is still only half tamed. Here are rocky hills, brushy pastures, and rude stone walls overgrown with poison ivy. Many of the homes are ancient and dilapidated and the premises strewn with careless litter. Work is carried on in a primitive fashion. A landowner of this district with whom I talked affirmed that farming did not pay, and the reason he gave was the competition of the West—it had knocked the bottom out of prices.

I wondered if there were not other reasons. He was furrowing out a half-acre patch on which he intended to plant potatoes. His hired man was leading the horse while he himself held the plough-handles. It seemed to me his patch was not large enough to work economically with a view to a profit, and that the profit was also being dissipated by having two men do work that might be done by one. Down the slope was a long stretch of marshes that swept away to the sea, with a muddy-banked creek wandering through the level. The man said he would cut salt hay on these marshes later in the year, and as the soil was too boggy to bear the weight of a horse, not only would the mowing have to be done by hand, but he and his helper would be obliged to carry the hay to firm land between them on poles. Here, again, it was not easy to discern much chance for profit. The process was too laborious where the product was of so little value. Then, at the man's home, I noted that the stable manure lay leaching in the sun and rain, unprotected by any roof, that the mowing-machine and other tools were scattered about the yard accumulating rust, and that things in general looked careless and easy-going. I did not wonder he took a pessimistic view of farming.

The places of many of his neighbors were akin to his, and as a whole this outlying district seemed a piece out of the past when farming was done by main strength, and brains and method and science were quite secondary. This old-fashioned aspect was further emphasized by the presence of an occasional slow ox-team toiling in the fields, and now and then an antiquated well-sweep in a dooryard.

A well-sweep was an adjunct of one house in the town itself—a gray, square little house far gone in decay. Lights were missing from the windows, clapboards were dropping off, blinds were dilapidated or gone altogether, and the outbuildings had either fallen and been used for stove wood, or were on the verge of ruin. The shed used as a hen-house leaned at a perilous slant. Near it was a scanty pile of wood and a sawhorse made by nailing a couple of sticks crosswise on the end of a box so that the tops projected above the box level and formed a crotch. Along the street walk staggered a decrepit picket fence with a sagging gate. The yard was a chaos of weeds and riotous briers, and the place looked mysterious—as if it had a history—perhaps was haunted.

A tiny path led around to the back door, so slightly trodden I was in doubt whether the house was inhabited or not until I saw a bent old woman coming from the grass field at the rear of the premises. On her head she wore a sunbonnet of ancient type and over her shoulders a faded shawl. She was hobbling slowly along with the help of a cane, and bore on her arm a basket with a few dandelion greens in the bottom. I stood leaning on the fence, hoping chance would give me an opportunity to know more about this strange house; and to avoid an appearance of staring I now looked the other way. But my loitering had attracted the woman's attention, and, instead of going into the house, she set her basket on the back door-step and came feebly down the path and spoke to me. She was a mild-eyed, kindly old soul, and in the chat which followed I learned that she was eighty years old and that her brother, aged seventy-six, the only other member of the household, was a "joiner." Presently I asked about some of the garden flowers which had survived in their neglected struggle with weeds and brambles.

"They need the old woman," she said, "but I'm most past such work now. My lameness is getting worse. I have it every winter, and it doesn't leave me until warm weather comes. I shall have to get my brother to hoe some here. He isn't much for taking care of flowers, but he likes 'em as well as any one, and if he's going to make a call, he'll pick a bunch to carry along. I used to have more kinds, and I'd keep some of 'em in the house through the winter, but when I did that I had to see the fire didn't go out nights, and it got too hard for me." ...

I was made welcome to step inside the house and see the old dwelling, but I did not find it especially interesting. The barren, cluttered rooms, with their suggestion of extreme poverty, were depressing. In the parlor, which was used as a sort of storeroom, were a number of antiquated pictures on the walls, most of them in heavy frames that the woman had contrived herself-some of cones, some of shells stuck

189

in putty. The cones and shells varied much in size and kind, and the patterns were intricate and ingenious. Then there was a specimen of hair work, dusty and moth-eaten, which she took out of its frame that I might inspect it closer. "I used to be quite a hand making these sort of things," she explained, "but now I don't have the time. It's about all I can do to get enough to eat."

I came away wondering what the trouble was that the brother and sister were so poorly provided for in their old age, and when I inquired about it I was told that the brother was "one of the smartest men in Connecticut," an architect and builder of great ability, but "he had looked through the bottom of a glass too often."

❧ JONATHAN DANIELS ❧

Jonathan Daniels understood the American South. He was the son of Josephus Daniels, the editor of the Raleigh (North Carolina) News and Observer, *who also served as Woodrow Wilson's Secretary of the Navy. A graduate of the University of North Carolina, the younger Daniels published in 1938 an insider's account of life in the region that was praised by reviewers because of its candid treatment of the race issue. This volume,* A Southerner Discovers the South, *was the product of a full year of travel and interviewing in all parts of Dixie.*

Daniels had no special knowledge of New England. When he journeyed north to investigate a part of the country far removed geographically and culturally from his native South, he came, not as an expert, but as an admitted outsider, a role that he characterized as an "inquisitive itinerant." He hoped that his status as a stranger would enable him to "see things which lie unnoticed (or at least unmentioned), beneath the native's nose." Daniels brought with him more than a comparative perspective; he was a skilled journalist who was not content with cur-

sory impressions but asked fundamental questions. "I was anxious to know what New England meant to itself and to America" he stated in the preface of A Southerner Discovers New England, *from which the sections below are taken.*

The 38 year old Daniels ventured into Connecticut twice during 1940. The first time he drove through the state on the recently opened Merritt Parkway on his way from New York City to upper New England. Later in the summer he returned for extended visits to New Haven and Hartford. His picture of Connecticut is far from flattering. He is sensitive to issues of class and race that fragmented this tiny state that was in the process of moving out of the Depression into wartime prosperity. Although he praises the airplane industry for preserving traditional Yankee ingenuity and skill, he is suspicious of the state's growing dependence on arms production.

H.J.

1940 The road runs into Connecticut through the middle of the world. The rock walls run in a procession of aching backs to the American beginning, and tractors pull open the furrows in the fields those backs bent to clear. There is solitude for a singer and her high notes on a hill; there is rest for the broker, quiet for the writer, and, for the painter, stretches of countryside undisturbed and unentered by the mixed multitude which crowds the state's square miles. Machines go on endlessly punching out the brass buttons. Test pilots take the new planes up over Bridgeport, high above the solemn stone over Barnum. Young women make corsets for old women. In peace and with precision the bullets are made that will tear the guts out of a man. A gymnasium which looks like a cathedral backs up in New Haven to a dark yard where boys play ball beside a huge garbage heap where first base ought to be. Czechoslovakians dwell in early American salt-box houses,

Excerpted from Jonathan Daniels, *A Southerner Discovers New England*, New York, Macmillan, 1940 and American boys go to college in medieval palaces. And yet there is order and content; there might even be security if the rich land like the rich men were not surrounded by a hungry world.

The hungry world, near and far, is not readily seen. A century ago Lucian Minor wrote home to Virginia, "Here is not apparent a hundredth part of the abject squalid poverty that our state presents." It is still so. It was simpler to see the young men of Yale than the equal number of young men and women in New Haven who could not find a job. As I entered New England the educated Negro who was still a filling station helper told me: "The Merritt Parkway is merely the Connecticut continuation of the New York parkway."

It is more than that; it is also the gate of New England and with other parkways will one day be a wide canal for cars cut straight through from Broadway to Boston. White lanes of concrete and miles of pretty planting provide the motorist every facilitation to motion; here is avenue of escape from both traffic and reality. One, I suspect, may sometimes be as objectionable as the other. This is progress, and it is also a million dollar parable on progress.

Instead of Connecticut, the rider sees mile after mile of identical right of way prettified with a million dollars' worth of grass and tree. When I rode it, the parkway was twenty-one miles of changeless green procession which looked all the way like those sentimentalized stoneless cemeteries which have made burial a real estate business and added to the economic hazards of quarrying in Vermont. Connecticut escaped the showing and I the seeing of the hamburger and the clam stands, the dine-and-dances, the tourist homes and the automobile graveyards. Maybe this was pure gain. I am not sure. For the man whose only interest in travel is the end of his journey here is perfection. Also served are those who have insisted that New England must be saved from the hot-dog salesman. But I rode as one who wanted not only to go but to see, and as one to whom a hot-dog stand was as much an item in a civilization as a transplanted spruce. This may be heresy. I think it makes as much sense as the doctrine: In order that the traveler may move in this land, he must give up the privilege of seeing it.

"He can have this business," the skinny man said. Behind the counter of his clam stand on the road from Westport to New Haven, he put down the bottle of his own beer which he had been drinking. He pushed my clams across the counter. "God knows he's welcome to it."

I had spoken casually about roadside stands of Connecticut.

"There are lots of stands on this road. When you first get off the parkway you realize how many there are."

"Too damn many."

"There's a professor at Yale who says Connecticut has got to get them off the roads if it expects to get the tourists."

My host sneered.

"He can have this business." He looked as if he meant to put the professor forcibly into the clam business. Then his face softened in self-pity. "Christ, all I got's clams! They're good all right, but I've had so many of them that they make me sick. They'll be fine for you, but I've had too many. I got to eat here, and that's about all I get. It's pretty damned easy for college professors to say how pretty things ought to be. But what about us poor bastards? I don't want to sell clams. I hate the sight of the damn things. And I get sick at the stomach watching automobiles riding this road. If they don't like to see me, God knows I don't get any fun out of seeing them. I get so sometimes I don't want any of them to stop. Let 'em keep their damn dimes." He paused. "How 'bout some more? They're good and fresh. A fellow brings 'em to me who digs 'em hisself."

"No, thanks."

"How 'bout a beer?"

"No."

"You been riding a long way," he said, looking at my license. "I got a brother went down South last winter. He ran a Kiddy Ride in a carnival. He liked it. He said the girls were nice, real nice. But I guess he was bragging. Pretty often he is."

"Maybe not," I said. "I guess I will have a beer."

He opened it.

"He liked it. I hear a lot of people talking about the South. Some of 'em say the South's going to take our factories away. Don't you believe it. One thing we got up here is skill. You can find fellows right around here that can do anything. That means a lot. I know some of these rich so-and-sos would move their mills to save a nickel. But we got the skill and they know it. Hell, I'm not worried!"

I put down my bottle.

"How 'bout some more clams? They're real good today. I had some myself just before you came."

Though the elms were hardly beginning to be green, old Connecticut was good to see: the stone walls, the white houses with the green blinds, the churches and their spires, and the Common and the Town Hall. The familiar picture of New England was a real picture on a real road. But the characters were different. The Italians and the Poles, the Jews and the Irish move at home on the Yankee scene. ...

I rode on. There were big trucks on the road with me now, roaring past me down out of New England and Connecticut with tin and silver and brass. There was a boxed airplane engine in a truck parked before a church. At Wallingford like a grim specter a huge "For Sale" sign hung against an old factory's wide brick wall. It was the first such mill I saw in New England, and I remembered a book published when more of us were young called *Get-Rich-Quick Wallingford*. It was possible now to become poor quick, too. Even on this crowded road.

"Don't you believe it," the clam-stand man had said of moving factories. On the rich road where he stood there seemed certainly to be no basis for fear. I remembered, however, that Malcolm Keir of Dartmouth, who had been economic adviser to the New England Governors' freight-rate committee, had used those same words to New England manufacturers, but in warning. There had been losses in textiles and knitting and shoes and leather and paper. Any manufacturer who believed that textile machinery could not follow textile manufacturing or other capital goods industries go after other consumers' goods industries (machine making after the products of machines) was, he suggested, a man riding on a pretty parkway who could not see the world.

"Don't you believe it," Malcolm Keir said.

The men in Meriden apparently did. At least those pouring out of the factories in the late afternoon were as complacent-looking as they seemed well fed. In their American working clothes I could not pick out diverse foreign stocks. As a crowd they looked as American as the factories from which they came. And, wherever they came from, they were. I stood on the sidewalk and let them move by me. One workman was talking about a golf score. A woman said to another, "She can't do that to me." The last man came out smiling and talking to the watchman at the doors. He knew they would open again in the morning.

I came into Hartford under the shadow of the high tower of the Travelers Insurance Company which wears at its top some decoration that looks at a distance like pawnbrokers' balls. In the Bond Hotel I talked with Willard Rogers, who not only runs the hotel but had the official job of talking for publicity for Connecticut.

"He's a B.W.— a Big Wind," said an insurance executive, "an Elk." (As a matter of fact, I don't think he is an Elk; but aristocratic Governor Saltonstall of Massachusetts is.)

I found him in his office, fat and fifty, immaculately and a little sportily dressed, with his little remaining hair brushed over his bald head. His fingernails were shining, I noticed when he moved his hand and the long cigar in it in gesticulation. He is expansive about Connecticut. Polyglot the people may be (thirty nationalities work in his hotels), but they are homogeneous in a sweet reasonableness which extends from the textile workers in hardship in eastern Connecticut through Hartford and the busy Connecticut River valley to New York.

"We don't have any crime. Even when we have strikes—of course the strikers want to win, but we don't have any violence unless outsiders come in and cause it. I was police commissioner of my town of Manchester for twenty years and we never did have but two murders. One of them was a China-man who was killed by an outsider in a tong war. The other case was a man killed in a duel over a girl which two Italians from Hartford came to Manchester to fight."

"Does that apply to all New England?"

"No," he said regretfully. ... "We don't have anything like that in Connecticut. The people are peaceful and reasonable and law-abiding."

I went back to my room, contemplating the productive peace in Babel. From my window I looked out across its capital and my eye fell to a legend printed on the sill:

NOTICE
Persons throwing bottles or
other articles from this win-
dow will be held responsible.
PLEASE
Be Careful

It was still possible that something might hit the sweetly reasonable below.

The Congregational Church was neither antique nor modern. It belonged to that age of golden-oak interiors, of yellow carved beams, of yellow pews, of yellow pulpit, even yellow walls. North and South, there seems to have been a period when such was the standard coloration of Christianity. Inside the church I might have been in Selma, Alabama, or Clarinda, Iowa. And not only the woodwork. The high-piled menu prepared under the direction of Miss Mary Smith with the assistance of Luces and Bigneys and Fosters and Hulberts conformed to a national church supper standard. When behind me the minister's voice rose in blessing it was not a New England voice but that theological seminary intonation which everywhere seems to me to make a contribution to Christianity similar to that made by golden oak. We ate heartily, plied by the ladies. The three school-teachers across the table from me were pretty and shy. The retired professional bicycle rider, whose father had been the town's leading surgeon, was a man of information. At the foot of the table sat the frail old man who occupied the highest house on the hill above it; he was the undertaker. They were an old American company, a familiar and not very exciting one. They ate placidly toward the beginning of the scheduled spelling match.

There was a difference here. In this church was the tradition of New England. The line had come down straight to them from the beginning. And not only the succession. They still held the wealth and the library and the schools and the social position. But outside the church the law was in the hands of an Irish chief of police named Joe McCarthy. A man named Howard headed the tree replacement committee but the trees were being planted for the numerous progeny of the Dombroskis and the Zacowiches and the Ratzenoffs. Nick DeRita had just bought the abandoned Stafford Street School. ...

In north Connecticut on the road to Worcester I could see the lick New England had been hit when the wind roared up out of the South. The hurricane had not broken the trees; it had followed rain, which had softened the earth, to push them down. Their roots were turned up in the air. An old buggy still hung in the wreckage of a barn. Not only the old trees had come down. I stopped at a store in the town of Union (settled 1727). Two selectmen there were Dorotzak and Mrakevich.

A wind has been changing New England for a long time. ... I lay in bed in New Haven and read the paper. There was a lot of New England news in it. ... Outside over New Haven the towers of Yale stuck up beyond the Green.

Old Eli had grown mightily with the money of Harkness and Sterling. It had more than five thousand students, and it paid professors five and a half million dollars to teach them everything from early Assyrian to advanced otolaryngology. Its Gothic architecture spread from the slums to the Green. Its Harkness Tower rose to the points of its crown beneath the sky. I had gone beneath it with the best guide in New Haven, Dr. James Rowland Angell, the first non-Yale man to be the president of Yale and the man under whom the old university had grown most in stone and dollars and students since its beginning.

I got such a guide by Southern luck: the scholar from Burlington, Vermont, who had come to the presidency of old Eli from the University of Chicago and who was the President Emeritus, had had the wisdom to marry a lovely lady from North Carolina. She sent me welcome to New Haven. When I came she was away on some good works she was doing; but Dr. Angell gave me good sherry, good luncheon, and good talk in the house on Blake Road which seems secluded in the center of a suburban block like a house in a forest. After luncheon he took me to see the great new brick and stone body of the old university. The former president, who was educated in Michigan, and the rich Harknesses from Ohio, and James Gamble Rogers, the architect from Kentucky, had built wisely in New England for both learning and beauty.

A greater Yale had to be built. Dr. Angell came with the wave of boys who followed the war into the colleges. The great American middle class, Dr. Angell told me, had seen that in the World War only the college boys got into the officers' training camps. That taught a lesson that was multitudinously learned. Since it is the essence of American democracy that everybody who has enough to eat wants to be an officer, the young cramped campuses everywhere. Yale was swollen with students who taxed its treasury and its walls. So the detail of the cathedral, the line of the chateau, the spirit of the early Congregational Church grew in New Haven beside the old brick buildings to make a remarkable congruity. The lady of a famous librarian planted shrubs shrewdly about new buildings to soften the appearance of swiftness in their emergence. Endowment went up like the Harkness Tower. And though young Stover of Yale, who now must be an old man in the pages of his adventures, probably would not approve, the story of the elders is that youth has grown more serious in New Haven and less collegiate. Say it softly: Even Skull and Bones and Wolf's Head and Scroll and Key, like the old gray mule, ain't what they used to be.

We went first to the beautiful Sterling Divinity Quadrangle, within the Georgian Colonial bounds of which it ought not to be difficult for anybody to be religious. The open court within the buildings of brick with white trim looked like a cloister for Congregationalists. It is not necessary now to be a Congregationalist to walk its ways. I wondered what the Christian purpose was in requiring a recent photograph of applicants for admission, but I did not wonder very much. I remember that, as we walked in the cloistered quadrangle, there was a woman's hairpin on the ground. Girls can become Bachelors of Divinity, too.

I did not like the Sterling Law Buildings so well. There is an ecclesiastical opulence about its brick and limestone Gothic which the satirical lunettes of lawyers do not quite offset. Though I knew that some of the conservative members of the Yale Corporation did not delight in the high New Deal content of the Yale Law School, it seemed odd to expect liberalism to flourish where so much wealth had accumulated around the boys and the books. We went on past the big gym that looks like a cathedral and the old chapel which looks like a barn, out to the monument to our times which is the Yale Bowl. Then we came back through the streets where the new undergraduate colleges are and to the old campus and the old buildings beyond the grass and the trees which, perversely perhaps, I liked best. Also I remember the pleasant court in the great Sterling Library where in the fountain bronze boys held between their legs fishes from which the water comes. The effect at a little distance for a nearsighted man is interesting. And I think the effect for anybody is an indication that the Puritan tradition has not been altogether lost.

The great university all together is lovely in the sun; but it seemed warmer and truer at night with the lights on in the windows where the boys were studying (and where I noticed that there were pennants on the walls, despite the report that the collegiate attitude is passing; I suspect that if I could have looked closer I should have seen pictures of movie stars). But Yale is not New Haven by day or by night. It is not quite true, as one New England newspaperman told me, that New Haven is "three-fourths slum and one-fourth Yale." There is, nevertheless, a hunger in New Haven which Yale does not fill. And, though it seems a little sad, the University, grown to wealth and greatness in New Haven, not long ago felt impelled to present its case in print to New Haven taxpayers and taxgatherers and quote a local tool manufacturer, educated at Iowa State College, to the effect that the University is a "going concern."

As much as Fall River does, or Manchester, New Haven wants to add new industries to the corset manufacturing on Derby Avenue (I wondered later if corset styles that Paris decreed that summer helped), to Winchester arms, to hardware, and to clocks. This is natural, but I am afraid it indicates what seemed indicated elsewhere, that New England in general is not aware that the education business is one of the best industries of New England. ...

Yale looked so big and bountifully solvent that there was some sentiment in the town around it to make it pay a big share of the town's taxes. The movement was serious enough for the University to print a little book about it which showed that Yale and its officers and business agencies were already paying a million dollars in scholarships and aids to New Haven students and direct contributions to the city. Furthermore, it had an annual pay roll of $5,508,000; it had spent an average of $3,600,000 for fifteen years in building operations; it was buying every year $2,695,000 in supplies. It estimated that its students and their friends spent $2,721,000 a year in the town. It added up its direct and indirect contributions to New Haven to a grand total of $15,383,375.69 a year. The total is probably more now. ...

(The Federal wages and hours law that spring provided a minimum wage of $11 a week. If the worker was employed every week, that would be $572 a year. But not all workers worked every week. Too many did not work at all. Many made more.) Yale told its prospective students: "With respect to total costs, $1,000 a year is probably a minimum; the average for boys who are working a substantial part of their way is $1,200 and the average for boys who receive all of their expenses from home is $1,600. These figures do not include travel or vacation expenses." There were then in New Haven, Homer Borst, head of the Community Chest, told me, as many unemployed young men and women between the ages of sixteen and twenty-five as the whole number of the students at Yale. Undoubtedly from a national point of view they are not as important as the young in the colleges being trained, as Yale says, for leadership. Yale is now cosmopolitan, and seeking to be more so with special scholarships for the best students from distant states. New Haven is polygot with 40,000 Italians, 30,000 Jews, 20,000 first and second generation Irishmen, 5,000 Negroes, Poles, other peoples. The young in New Haven sought jobs, not leadership; but they sought jobs and did not find them in a city in which leadership had been a professed product since the college came from Saybrook in 1716. ...

When I went into the New Haven Community Chest office, Mr. Borst was talking on the phone. ...He is a gray-haired, middle-aged man, a little distrustful, I think, of itinerant writers and questioners, and probably no more so than he ought to be. But he told me the striking comparison between the learning young and the unemployed young. I wanted to find out about them and their mothers and fathers and sisters and brothers. What was the sum of relief expenditures that supported them in a city like New Haven; What did the

Community Chest plus municipal relief expenditures plus WPA plus other forms of relief add up to?

Mr. Borst considered my question in an approximation of amazement which it may have deserved. If I would stay there a month, he said, I could work it up. He was not very hopeful of my making any sense in less time than that. They had the statistics, they had a statistician. But they had not tabulated them. What good were they untabulated, I wondered. He explained to me very patiently that I was asking the impossible, and he took me back to let the lady statistician explain. I am sure they must have been right. I remembered that when I came back from Europe in the middle of the depression to work on *Fortune*, all the big businesses in downtown New York had huge statistical departments. They had all the facts, but these did not add up to anything. Maybe the expansion of knowledge in continuing confusion applied even to the bigger Yale. Mr. Borst gave me copies of his annual reports. They seemed admirable, particularly a statement in the last one: "To state that $602,709 was subscribed in the last campaign does not say anything. We need to see this sum in perspective." I still think that's right.

Outside on Elm Street a policeman had been putting tickets on too long parked cars and singing, "Sweetheart of mine, I love you." Now as I came out there was brassier music coming from under the elms across the Green. Before Center Church the listening, looking crowds were already lined up to see part of the pageantry in which Benedict Arnold (still in the role of hero) was to demand for the 164th time the keys to the Powder House. The Yale boys and the Negroes, the Italians and the Poles and the Irish in the crowds knew he would get them from the selectmen, but they waited in expectancy while the notes of "Onward, Christian Soldiers" roared up the Green from the horns of the band of the Governor's Footguards. The big clock in the church tower belled three. Then came the police of New Haven on motorcycles and marching with their clubs held like sabers. They took their places on each side of an elderly clergyman in red-caped black gown who waited on the church steps. The Governor in shining top hat came in a limousine. Then the Governor's Footguards came marching under their hot, foot-high bearskin shakos (I think that is the name). The Footguards were gentlemen in an age in which most gentlemen are sedentary. As soldiers they did not look very formidable. I remember one man who still looked like a professor peering nearsightedly through his pince-nez glasses as he marched in determination under his tall fur hat. All of them in their old-fashioned uniforms looked less like soldiers than like well-to-do middle-aged men whose wives had gotten them into costumes for a ball. But they marched. A bugle blew.

"Christ," said a plebeian behind me in the crowd, "some gob would 'a' done better than that."

"They ought to go to camp for about six weeks."

"What the hell! It's more of a social gathering than anything else."

The Footguards halted. A plumed officer grinned at his men.

"He ought to laugh," said another of the commentators in the crowd. "The Boy Scouts do better than that."

The officer, a florid man in a cocked hat with blue and white feathers, got a cigarette out of his colonial uniform and lit it. He dragged on it gratefully. A command came from his superior on the church steps. He threw his cigarette down and echoed the command. The clergyman and the Governor, the Footguards and the policemen all moved into the church with the flags bringing up the rear. Only the Yale field artillery unit of the R.O.T.C. remained outside. They took, grinning, the taunts of other unmilitary Yale boys. But the regular army sergeant kept his eyes on his fieldpieces, unamused and grim.

The crowd dispersed slowly, and I went on to the Taft Bar to meet a friend who told me about the teachers' union in Yale. Not even all the learned felt secure. Later he sent me a clipping about the union at Harvard which contained a union statement that "teachers are not fungible goods." "Fungible" is a learned legal word meaning, I gather, interchangeable. It is true, and not only true of teachers. Just north of

where we sat drinking, Eli Whitney, who fixed the economy of the South
with his cotton gin, had profoundly altered even Connecticut with his
use of interchangeable parts in manufacturing which is the basis of mass
production. North and south, even within the limits of New Haven,
people persisted in being infinitely different and diverse. One professor
of paleontology was better than another one; on Derby Avenue one woman
was more skilled than another at making corsets. But there are hungers
and fears which run through them all, through the neurophysiologist
as well as the needleworker. Yale rises in New England and helps light
the world, but there remain dark places close to its edges in the
town, maybe even in the Gothic corners of its own halls. There may
be a shadow even under a torch....

The bell was continually ringing. A determinedly gay man in his late
forties, paunchy and vacant-faced, kept pulling the string that rang the
bell on the automobile costumed as a French locomotive and cab
which sat parked on Asylum Street. He grinned at passers-by mechanically and went on ringing his bell mechanically. I recognized him and
his train before I read the sign: "Quarante Hommes et Huit Chevaux."
My older brother had been one of the Horses and Men, and I knew the
uniform. The veterans were gathering for meeting in Hartford. At the
door of the Bond Hotel, two uniformed men were worrying out loud about
the late arrival of the band. There were more veterans in the hotel in
uniform, and with them one strikingly handsome man in a wheel
chair. It was easy to see that he was important. Two very pretty women
came across the lobby to speak to him. As I passed them I noticed that
the handsome man in the chair had no legs at all.

I had come into Hartford by Farmington, a lovely town at a lovely
time. The dogwood was in bloom and the magnolia, and a stand beside
the road advertised not only fresh-cut asparagus and broilers but pie:
apple or lemon. There was one apple tree lying on the ground where
the wind had blown it, but nevertheless in full white bloom; and, being

never wholly the aesthete, I wondered if its beautiful blossoms would ever grow to fruit and pie. Grand fat cattle munched the grass in that combination of steady activity and complete leisure which seems possible only in cows. There were lilacs. An old sleigh stood in the green yard of an antique shop. As I came into Farmington I met a company of horseback riders, among them a blonde girl wearing green breeches and a yellow coat. The picket fences were white, and there were ancient dates on the houses. In a field in the midst of the old houses were more cattle, and in another field two boys, with model airplanes almost as big as themselves, were preparing for a flight. In the old town kept sweet for the secure in the present, they were, I knew, part of the same Connecticut tradition which builds and tests the roaring airplane engines and bright aluminum propellers beyond the capital in East Hartford.

There was no war then. The nagging threat of it was no sharper than it had been in the months before; but the world was moving to war, and Frederick B. Rentschler, chairman of the board of the United Aircraft Corporation, spoke from the facts when he indulged in the prophecy "that 1939 shipments will be the largest in our history." In 1938 the shipments had risen to $36,800,000 from beginning in a tobacco warehouse without any orders in 1925. It was not the war that interested me then. A good deal of man's modern movement had begun in Connecticut. The bicycle had begun in America in Hartford. Automobiles had been made there. Both rolled in possibility upon Charles Goodyear's invention of the process of vulcanizing rubber not far from Hartford in Naugatuck, just a hundred years before I rolled on his invention into Hartford and across the Connecticut River to the United Aircraft plants. But in recent years the bicycle had been left behind. The automobile had moved West. Aviation was something new and precious in the tradition in which they began. Aviation plants in East Hartford and Bridgeport are counted as details of national power by the generals and the statesmen; but in New England before war they meant a new industry in a region which was clinging, precariously sometimes, to old ones. They meant, also, trib-

ute to the New England faith in the New England skill, and jobs which
even in fortunate Hartford have been as welcome as needed.

"During a little less than fifteen years," said Mr. Rentschler, who was
born in Ohio, "we have grown steadily to a point where our original per-
sonnel has been expanded into an average force of between 5,000 and
6,000 people, with a pay roll approaching a million dollars monthly. We
have given employment to the very finest type of mechanics and
skilled workmen, at highest wages. We have always been extremely satisfied with our location in New England, and particularly in Hartford,
principally because of the availability there of the skilled labor which
is so necessary for our operations, as well as the facilities which it offers
for the procurement of materials and even manufacturing assistance from
many of the other skilled workshops of New England. We believe that
we must have been a considerable factor against unemployment in Hartford
and Connecticut, particularly during the last five or six years."

The offices of the plant in East Hartford sit behind a green lawn in
an unimpressive-looking building. I went to them with a telegram from
President Donald Brown (born in Wisconsin), saying I was welcome to
come and see. The little anteroom at the door was crowded with people who looked like salesmen hoping to sell and job hunters hoping to
get bought. I waited while the telephone operator called, and at last,
a slim, pleasant young man in white linens came out. He was E.L. Eveleth.
He gave me passes to sign. I had to be an American citizen. (Foreigners
could only get in with the help of the air attaches of their embassies and
the approval of the War, State, and Navy departments.) I was No. B24049
on a blue pass to the Pratt & Whitney engine factory and No. 10971 on
a red pass to the Hamilton Standard Propeller factory. ...

Eveleth took me out through a garage and a locked door into the engine
factory. I wore my pass on my coat. We moved past guards in a huge room.
In a real sense it was an assembly plant since most of the engine parts
were forged and cast elsewhere and shipped in. But the mass production lines of the automobile plants are not duplicated. More care is nec-

essary, more skill. If a Ford breaks down south of Cincinnati it can be pulled into a garage. If an airplane engine stops turning above Saarbrucken, or on an air-line route in Colorado, it may be a different and sadder story. Certainly the men finishing and assembling the engine parts looked like skilled workmen doing skilled work. (Women were used only for packing small spare parts and for inspection in which they have a reputation for a patience superior to men's.)

"There's millions' worth of machine tools in this plant," Eveleth said. They came from Worcester, Providence, Hartford (United Aircraft grew from the combination of the spare money and spare space of the Niles Bement & Pond Company, Pratt & Whitney division, the old Hartford machine tool makers. It grew also around Rentschler, Brown, and George J. Mead, the one New Englander of the trio, who had seceded from the Wright Aeronautical Corporation in New Jersey to form a company of their own.) There were tools from the Middle West. I particularly remember one beautiful gear cutter made by a Middle Western firm which bore the name of a woman who had designed the machine.

One man assembles a whole engine: That means both responsibility and skill. But certainly he does not do a one-man job. There is as vast and varied an assistance behind him as behind the single aviator who takes the controls of the strong, clean completed plane. He only stands at the bottleneck of tools and foundries and laboratories putting together the products of a technical civilization for such a roaring mechanism of power as means speed or fury. The product he puts together costs something like $12 to $15 per horsepower, and there are plenty of 1,000 horsepower engines with more power in one of them than the whole company of the settlers of Hartford had in themselves and their stock when they came over from Cambridge, Massachusetts, in 1635.

And they roar: We went out big doors to the noisy space before the thundering testing rooms. In each room engines were set up and running, and despite the heavy brick walls and big thick wooden doors about them, the noise was terrific. They made a power which was designed to fling wings across the sky, but all their monster droning ... was for men behind plate-glass windows who, with rubber guards against the roar in their ears, watched the motors hours long, watched dials, and recorded every reading on every phase of performance on special sheets by five- or ten-minute intervals. Afterward the movement of a man's hand would make all their power silent. Men would take them all apart again and then put them together for final tests. In big boxes they go to Bridgeport where in the Vought-Sikorsky plane plant of the company they provide the power that rides the sky.

Propellers might seem an anticlimax after engines. They did not seem so to me. Next door to the engine factory the Hamilton Standard Propeller plant occupies the whole space the Chance-Vought Airplane Company used before it moved to Bridgeport. ...I was aware that propellers were no longer the mere revolving wooden blades they had been when flying began; but I did not know that hundreds of parts are required in a propeller alone, and that one propeller may cost $3,000. They are beautiful things which emerge from the raw, rough-shaped slabs of aluminum alloy almost as a statue comes out of the stone. Indeed, I had the feeling that what workmen did with aluminum and steel in these plants was more aesthetic as well as more precise and utilitarian than what I had seen other skilled men doing with silver in Providence.

They were making beautiful things, even if, as some men said, the arms makers were the war makers. ...

The present company of workers look excellent certainly. By no means all of them are descended from the Connecticut Yankee. The skilled trades of New England depend, as the unskilled trades do, upon all the complexity of immigrant stocks which have come in; but I wondered, remembering the father that had spoken of a son in aviation, if the Nantucket whaler's son's boy was in one of the big halls shaping the twist of a propeller, assembling the parts to make an engine's power, standing at a window and watching the imprisoned roar of 1,000 horsepower in a testing room. Here was work for men in a New England in which jobs for

The Connecticut Historical Society, Hartford.

"...more aesthetic as well as more precise and utilitarian than what I had seen...men doing with silver..."

—Jonathan Daniels

men were less and less available in the cities where the garment factories and novelty companies had come to fill emptiness. Here was needed the old combination of strength and skill.

And of youth. The old man of United, Chairman Frederick Rentschler, brother of a machinery manufacturer in Ohio and of the president of the National City Bank of New York, was only fifty-one. President Brown was forty-nine. George Mead, the third of the technical trio who began the industry in Hartford, was forty-seven. There has been no time for old workers to grow around them. I remember young and very young-looking John Burridge, whose regular job is keeping airline maintenance men acquainted with factory methods. He went with us through the propeller plants. His young interest in the air was as bright and certain as the blades of the propellers he showed us. ...

I rode into town, from the newest New England to the oldest, to talk to a farmer who tells other farmers how to farm. He was disturbed over the temporary trouble of drought. The late spring had delayed the planting, and the lack of rain kept the seeds from sprouting. There were troubles beyond that spring. Connecticut farming had suffered long ago when the Erie Canal poured cheap food in from the West. Then the automobile had made part-time farming possible, and now the absence of horses in an automotive land made manure precious when manure was needed on the steadily cropped truck farms. The dairy farms needed their own manure. Taxes were high in the crowded land. The young Italians did not want to work on the farms.

Up the Connecticut valley there were human problems on the tobacco farms: The weed is usually grown as a one-crop specialty. The little one-family home-living New England farm is giving way, under demands for large amounts of capital and labor required to produce shade tobacco (whole fields look tented), to corporate farms. Cigar manufacturing companies own and operate their own huge places. Labor is often brought out by the truckload from Hartford. The independent yeoman was not having it easy in Connecticut.

In the late afternoon at Main Street and Central Row I looked up beyond the Travelers Insurance tower to a plane in the sky. None of the armies of insurance company clerks around me paid it any attention. They were headed like pigeons home to the suburbs, which have grown faster than the town. The aviator up there in the Connecticut sky, I thought, was independent. A whole technical civilization was behind him, rules surrounded him. But he was up there free with tremendous power under his hand. That would, of course, be an illusion: the power did not belong to him; his right to be a free man or a fool was more strictly limited than a Ford driver's. But the illusion was a great deal in a crowded world, more than a man can have working tobacco under a tent, or a woman sewing leaves on laths to be hung in the long barns. Maybe more than a clerk can have in an insurance tower. A woman bumped into me and told me to look where I was going. She was right, and so I took my eyes out of the sky.

I kept them on Hartford. I walked down Main Street and listened to street preaching to the street poor, "We are all sinners of Adam's race." I went back by the Bond Hotel and past it, following the sound of a carnival's calliope to a midway by the New York, New Haven & Hartford tracks and under the illuminated dome of the Capitol. In the flaring midway the biggest crowd of Connecticut Yankees were gathered before the suggestive gyrating of the Creole Belles, some very unattractive yellow colored girls. I followed the crowd in and sat down beside a big cripple who waited in contented lechery for the show.

"I always come the first night," he told me, "because they do things then to get the word around. There was a carnival over in East Hartford, and a girl had her tit out. I always go the first night. They do things then to get the word around."

I went back to the hotel. The Forty and Eight train was still at the door. There were veterans in the lobby. I looked among them but did not see again the clean, handsome man in the wheel chair. Later in my room, as I tried to go to sleep, the bell of the toy train kept sounding. I wondered if several rang it, or if it were rung so often by a never wearying hand. There was music around it, dance music which went on, scarcely ever stopping, for such veterans as still had legs.

There has been change in Hartford. The Morgan family which produced the J. Pierponts and built the pink granite Morgan Memorial museum will no longer sell you a cup of coffee, though it was around their cups in their coffee house that the insurance business began. They have moved away and done very well. Mark Twain, who complained that the Hartford city government had done him many a mean trick in sixteen years, is dead, and the reverent show his house, forgetting that he also said that irreverence is the champion of liberty and its only sure defense. Anne Royall is dead, too. She was an early journalist who worked under the name of Paul Pry. She came from Alabama to Hartford and reported: "The ladies of Hartford have a slight tinge of melancholy in their countenance; it is softened by a shade of placid tranquillity." Of all the dead I wish most that she could come back and see the ladies pouring into the insurance buildings in the mornings and out again at night.

Hartford, the patriotic there will tell you now, is the insurance capital of America. It is a good deal more than that. Actually it is the white-collar capital of the world which is more often than not better symbolized by a white and feminine throat. It is not only insurance which gives employment to armies of women in towers in Hartford as well as soft-handed gentlemen and swift-fingered girls across a continent. Hartford is the capital of those insurance agents everywhere who once were spoken of with no more kindness than still goes to Congressmen. In Hartford, also, more typewriters are made than anywhere else on earth. It is the machine upon which women everywhere rode to freedom or labor-I am not sure which. He was a neat Yankee god or one liking to make his caprice called progress very clear who put the clerical industry of insurance and the clerical engine of the typewriter side by side in the same Connecticut town.

The result is not a feminine town. There were, the last census said, more women than men in Connecticut. But the old Yankee surplus of Yankee spinsters disappeared before women went to work in such large numbers in the office buildings and the factories. In four New England states there were more women than men, there were also more women than men in six Southern states, and nowhere else in America. This may mean that the men are still leaving the older regions. I don't know. I do know that in Hartford the women work, and that in working in one way or another their activities touch lives all across the land. I went up Asylum Street toward Main early in the morning to see the girls gathering.

All of them were hurried, and some of them were pretty. There were two men walking in no hurry at all up and down before a shop with signs which charged that the proprietor was unfair to organized window cleaners. The women were washing windows no more. But they were pouring into the doors of the Travelers Insurance Company at 700 Main Street, the Aetna Fire at 670 Main. They would be filling doors, too, I knew, on Pearl and Elm and Cogswell and Trumbull streets. Out on Farmington Avenue they would be crowding the parking lots around the biggest colonial building in the world. Not all the women who came in from the spreading suburbs filed the papers on the risks and answered the letters of the agents. In a city in which one out of every seven humans is a woman working for her living, they also made typewriters at which other women would work, inspected arms with which men would kill, worked for Connecticut in the Capitol, and in season labored for the big corporate tobacco growers. Up Main Street, a woman ran the biggest store in Connecticut, G. Fox & Company, established 1847; Beatrice Auerbach ran it during a time of change which was putting women to work but also in which the coming together of the new Jews and Catholics made an emotional violence under the economic prosperity. And where there was pinch there was hate.

There is pinch. Occasionally it is dramatically displayed. I remember when I walked up the steps to the granite-columned porch of the beautiful building of *The Hartford Times* the view on my right held in the foreground the back porches of tenements not lovely to behold. On the porch of the templelike newspaper plant the architect had put, "News is an immortal bubble." And poverty, I thought, looking back at the tenements, is immortal even in the midst of prosperity. Where it exists, it ought not to be surprising if a priest in Michigan can stir anger in Connecticut. Just as in the South there is more than a casual connection between hunger and lynchings, so in New England anti-Semitism is economic, also.

In New England as in the South, the well-to-do of the old American stock are safe above the darker furies. They are even more remote, I think, in New England. The Yankees who rule the banks and the insurance companies and the mills are in large measure a race above and apart. The angry gentiles are themselves, at least in the cities, people of the immigrant stocks. The ancient Jews are a new people, too. In Hartford in recent years they multiplied around the few old Jewish families until the city had proportionately a larger number of Jews than any American community except New York or Atlantic City. In the same years the old group of full native American parentage decreased to scarcely more than a quarter of the people.

Still at the top the tradition of the Yankee goes on. It is a tradition full of charm, if also one based upon hardheadedness. For instance there is Morgan Brainard, president of the Aetna Life, whose place in the bright office beneath the tower which James Gamble Rogers designed for him depends upon his own lively intelligence, but who stands, nevertheless, in the blood line of the founder of the big company. Quiet, hospitable Charles C. Hemenway, editor of *The Times*, took me to see him. A tall man, gray and merry, Brainard rose to greet us. He took us out on the green roof garden beyond the wrought-iron porch at his office door. We could look back at the center of the city and down at the tennis courts of clay and of grass. I think there was also a bowling green. ...

We saw the table where the Aetna directors sit, which Aetna publicity says belonged to Thomas Jefferson. Mr. Brainard expressed a doubt that Jefferson ever saw it. He showed us an interesting old chime clock, an old-time lithograph of a very uplifting nonalcoholic barroom. He laughed, "All the really nice things in here belong to me, not the company." Down in the city I knew the business man with a sense of both history and humor had given the Avery Memorial museum the collection of old Connecticut inn signs which hang on its walls.

The hospitable Mr. Hemenway took me back to town to meet some of Hartford's men at the Hartford Club. ... I found the club and the company friendly and pleasant enough. Graham Anthony from North Carolina was there in his proper person as a Hartford manufacturer. Berkeley Cox, who taught me in prep school, was there as a counsel of the Aetna Life. The others might have been more awesome: two bank presidents; an insurance company president, the president of the big Niles Bement & Pond Company, a typewriter manufacturer, a big printer, Maurice S. Sherman, editor of the venerable *Hartford Courant*, a couple of other manufacturers, and the manager of the employment bureau of the Manufacturers Association of Hartford County. Altogether they made a powerful party. There were plenty of feet at which an inquisitive itinerant might sit and secure information. There were too many of them, and if they were not of clay, they were still feet to stand upon a common American earth. Above them the stories went around, masculine and hearty. If there is a rivet in the neck of the masters of Hartford, it has a hinge in it for laughter.

"I was thinking afterwards," my host, Hemenway, said, "that while this group was not the only one which could be assembled of which the same thing could be said, nevertheless it did typify what might be called the old school of Hartford philosophy about as well as any that could be gathered. Yet at least eight of the fourteen present came here from outside the state as mature men, most of them within twenty years or less. So the community impinges on the consciousness of those who come here from elsewhere to have part in managing affairs."

But, if old Hartford puts its pattern on the men at the top, men and women at the bottom are subject to influence from outside. The newspapers found that out when they casually criticized Father Coughlin. It was like setting off a storm. Whatever may have been the intentions of the pastor of the Shrine of the Little Flower, he stirred a storm which came in general from the Catholics in the direction of the Jews. The Catholics? Well, that is hardly fair. There are in Hartford, as elsewhere, a great many Catholics who are as tolerant as any Protestants —many, indeed, who know that Catholics themselves have suffered from the sharp end of intolerance. (The old fatuous Know-Nothing party flourished in New England; in Boston a convent was burned.) The truth is that North and South—and everywhere else—intolerance is most often the unintelligent or mislead expression of the exasperation of the poor. It happens that, in New England in general, the poor are Catholic. Coughlin stirs them only as Tom Watson, a Catholic baiter, stirred the violent intolerance of the poor Georgia Protestant whites. The poor who hate seem to me as sad as the pitiful who are hated. It is the seashore and schoolhouse anti-Semites who make me sick.

In Hartford the thing swelled up out of a secrecy in which it had spread from little mind to little mind. It rose in an avalanche of letters, anonymous and otherwise. The phones rang and rang and rang in the newspaper offices. An angry Irishman, someone told me, called up Maurice Sherman, editor of The Courant, and told him he could not pretend to be anything but "a damned Jew" with that name. (Sherman is a Congregationalist, a Son of the American Revolution, and was born in Yankee Hanover, New Hampshire.) More menacing, as its growth had been more secret, a movement of petitions began to come in from rural Windham County, from schoolteachers and farmers, protesting against the firing of gentile girls and replacing them with Jews in such big stores as Fox's. The petitioners had been lied to. No such thing had happened. Beatrice Auerbach, who is generally regarded not only as the Number One merchant of Connecticut but also as one of its best citizens, had the pay-roll sheets to show it. Sometimes the truth runs a poor race with a lie. Even when fury quiets, nobody knows how widespread intolerance remains. It begins in the dark. It works there. Its explosion waits for a spark.

The white-collar capital and the white-collar suburbs around it might be tinder for it. That white-collar mind extends to skilled workers in factories from their sisters in the offices. They certainly do not make any familiar proletariat. The unions had not made much headway in Hartford among the office workers. The tool makers and airplane makers were still unorganized. The real estate men and the chamber of commerce urged home ownership: 22 per cent of the people owned their own homes in Hartford. They needed very little urging to buy automobiles. It is the business of *The Hartford Courant* to know what the little folk of Connecticut want. It understood that they were afraid of death, even of being buried in one of those unobtrusive bits of meadow which Hendrik Willem van Loon reports, as new resident and new patriot, to be the most pleasant cemeteries in the world. I suspect *The Courant,* which has been reporting the news in Connecticut since October 1764, understands it better than the dearly loving Dutchman. At any rate it announced, during the summer I was in and out of Hartford, that "although it may be depriving its readers of a bit of information which they have been accustomed to find in the press, *The Courant* is now omitting to mention in its obituary columns the nature of the disease or ailment to which death was attributable ... If we can make through the policy here announced a small contribution to the peace of mind of those who foster gloomy predictions we shall be well satisfied ..." All day in offices the women work on the risks and rates of death from all its causes. Men make planes and pistols that conceivably may kill. Afterwards they run home to the suburbs. They have reason to know even better than the rest of us do that, no matter how long or how often the big insurance companies call it life insurance, this big item of Hartford's business remains death insurance just the same, and nothing else.

The state around their fears does look as sweetly tolerant as the appreciative Mr. van Loon, whose first faith is tolerance, sees it from his house under the elms in the Connecticut to which he, like a great many other authors and artists, has come from New York. (And besides, as Lily Pons and Peggy Wood said, the taxes are gentler on the artists.) Mr. van Loon said: "It may be the landscape that has made the people of this state a little more tolerant." In Hartford all the public patterns are tolerant. The schools are open for all—that is, the public schools (but many of the Catholic children do not attend them). Even the Negroes can get such an education in Hartford as not even a white child (who gets the lion's share of the school advantages) could get in the South. But beyond the schools: Relatively few Jews are employed by most of the big insurance companies in Hartford. There is "no prohibition as to race or creed"; neither are there many Jews. Negroes are rarely employed in any business operated by white people except as porters or messengers. (I remembered that I had been told in Providence that Negro graduates of the Rhode Island School of Design could only be placed as teachers in Negro schools to teach more Negroes who have no chance of employment except as teachers of other Negroes to ... If there ever was an example of what the colloquial call the "run around," here, it seemed to me, was it.)

Hartford is a pleasant city as well as a prosperous one. In the afternoon the big office buildings pour out their contented office workers. In the factories the typewriter makers stop preparing for more white-collar and white-throat workers in Hartford and far away. The insurance premium income pours into the town by the millions. The airplanes and the typewriters go out. The late-afternoon sun hits the gold leaf on the dome of the ugly Capitol. Hartford rests in content and confidence that it knows the risk on almost every aspect of American life and will not lose on any of them.

"Your South," an executive told me in the Bond Bar, "used to be the most incendiary region and the poorest risk in fire insurance; it's better now."

"That's good," I said. Through a wide door I watched young Hartford dancing in the next room. The boys and girls seemed both decorous and gay. But, looking at them, I wished someone in a city of actuaries could work out the risks to decency in their democracy from the bitterness and the fear that were out there somewhere still working in the dark.

THE ACORN CLUB
1899 – 1999

The centennial year of the Acorn Club is an appropriate time to review the Club's origin and purpose. Its Constitution states: "The club is organized for the purpose of issuing either as reprints or original publications rare printed books or early manuscripts, especially relative to Connecticut."

The Acorn Club was founded at a meeting on May 19, 1899 at The Connecticut Historical Society, then quartered, with the Watkinson Library in the Wadsworth Atheneum, Hartford. Frederick W. Skiff was named President; W.N.C. Carleton, Secretary; John Murphy, Treasurer; and Albert C. Bates, Editor. Charles N. Camp also attended as a founder.

Skiff, age 32, a book collector and author, was employed at the Connecticut Insurance Department in West Haven. By 1906 he had resigned and moved to Portland, Oregon. Carleton, age 26, a member until his death in 1943, was the Librarian of Trinity College. He continued his distinguished career as the Librarian of the Newberry Library, a noted humanities research library in Chicago. Murphy, age 24, is a mysterious member, a New Haven carriage maker, a Yale graduate (1897) who served as president of the Club from 1915 until his death in 1920. Bates, age 34, and a member until his death in 1954, served as Librarian of the Connecticut Historical Society from 1892 until 1940. A collector, author, and editor, he was conceivably the initiator of the Club, given the location of the first meeting. Camp, age 46 and a resident of New Haven was, according to his fragmentary biography, a genealogist, heraldic artist and possibly a teacher.

The Club chose as its first publication a very rare colonial imprint - Samuel Stone's *A Short Catechism*, printed by Samuel Green in Boston in 1684 for John Wadsworth of Farmington. It had been written many years before by Stone (1602-63) for the guidance of his First Church, Hartford congregation. Only two copies of the pamphlet were known at the time, one the George Brinley copy in the Watkinson Library. The Watkinson copy was used for the facsimile printed by Case, Lockwood and Brainard of Hartford. One hundred copies were produced, to be sold at two dollars per copy. Appropriately for the Charter Oak State, the pamphlet bore a wood engraving of an acorn, created by William F. Hopson of New Haven, who was to become a club member in the first year.

The fact that it took only two years to reach the prescribed limit of 25 members indicates that the founders had the membership well in mind from the outset. Scholarly in the broadest sense, the members included a wide variety of interests: artist, novelist, wood engraver, lawyer, mattress company president (later Governor of Connecticut), linen company president, Deputy State Comptroller, Watkinson Librarian, Connecticut State Librarian, retired State Librarian, Yale University Librarian, Wesleyan University Librarian, Yale Professor of History, Yale Professor and author, and Trinity Professor of History.

In 1999, with a cumulative roster far exceeding in numbers its hundred years, the Club's membership is still diversified: authors, architects, librarians, professors, historians, lawyers, and representatives of historical organizations. The Club has to its credit 34 publications relating to Connecticut history.

Extensive archives of the Club at the Connecticut Historical Society await a future historian. It has been my privilege, as an active member for almost half of its century (1953-99), to present this brief account of the Acorn Club's beginnings.

D. B.C.

CURRENT MEMBERS, JANUARY 1, 1999
(with initial dates of membership)

Elizabeth Brown, Guilford - 1997
Richard Buel, Jr., Essex - 1993
Christopher Collier, Orange - 1986
Milton P. DeVane, Hamden - 1997
Ralph Gregory Elliot, West Hartford - 1988
Donald B. Engley, Bloomfield - 1953
James F. English, Jr., West Hartford - 1981
Bruce Fraser, Middletown - 1988
Ellsworth S. Grant, West Hartford - 1986
William Hosley, Enfield - 1998
Oliver O. Jensen, Old Saybrook - 1976
David Kahn, Hartford - 1998
Howard R. Lamar, North Haven - 1998
Robert U. Massey, Avon - 1992
J. Bard McNulty, Glastonbury - 1980
David Franklin Musto, New Haven - 1987
William Robinson, Guilford - 1997
Brian Rogers, Mystic - 1986
Judith Ann Schiff, New Haven - 1995
John W. Shannahan, Hartford - 1998
Edward W. Sloan, Farmington - 1986
Gaddis Smith, New Haven - 1990
George J. Willauer, New London - 1998

Honorary Members
John M. K. Davis, Bloomfield - 1939
Marshall H. Montgomery, Del Ray Beach, FL - 1971
Willard M. Wallace, Berlin - 1961
Glenn Weaver, Wethersfield - 1964